# BECOMING AN EXTRAORDINARY LEADER
## Impacting Others to Lead

Dr. Jimmie Reed

BECOMING AN EXTRAORDINARY LEADER

Impacting Others to Lead

By Dr. Jimmie Reed

Copyright © 2006 by Dr. Jimmie Reed

Jimmie Reed Ministries
PO Box 63582
Colorado Springs, CO 80962

ISBN 978-1-615292-16-5

All rights reserved solely by the author. The author guarantees all contents are original and do not infringe upon the legal rights of any other person or work. No part of this book may be reproduced in any form without the permission of the author. The views expressed in this book are not necessarily those of the publisher.

Most scripture quotations, unless otherwise indicated, are taken from the King James Version.

# ENDORSEMENTS

༺◈༻

**"A Hands-on Book"**

Jimmie Reed has written a hands-on book about the kind of leadership that is needed within the Body of Christ today—containing basic, helpful and encouraging principles that will impact many and raise up tomorrow's generation of leaders. After reading it you will be challenged to become an extraordinary leader!

Quin Sherrer
Author
*"A Grandma's Prayer"*

**"A Must Read"**

Have you ever wondered how to get to the next level of meaningful leadership? If you are a person who wants to be a leader, is a leader-in-training, or an established leader, *Becoming an Extraordinary Leader* is a must read.

Dr. Jimmie Reed takes you from developing the fundamentals of leadership in your life to reproducing and releasing the next generation of leaders out of your life. *Becoming an Extraordinary Leader* is systematic, methodical, and practical instruction for becoming a person of influence and impact.

Calvin D. Brown
Founder and Chairman
Technically Inclined

## ACKNOWLEDGEMENTS

ഗ്രര്

*As I present this book I would like to acknowledge and thank the following special people who have blessed my life and helped make this project possible.*

To my children
LITA, MICHAEL, KENNETH AND JERMAINE

You have stood by me and encouraged me in the spiritual endeavors the Lord has for me. To each of you, I am grateful.

To BISHOP BILL HAMON
President, Christian International Apostolic
Network of Churches and Ministries

You model the principles taught in this book by teaching, training, equipping, and walking alongside those whom God has called you to lead.

To my spiritual parents Earl and Sara

You are examples of strong leadership in my life.

To ROXANNE RYAN
His Voice / His Pen Ministries

Many thanks to you for working diligently with me, assisting in the writing of this book.

To QUIN SHERRER
Author of *A Grandma's Prayers*

A special thanks to you, a friend who continues to inspire and encourage me to write.

To MY INTERCESSORS

Thank you for praying for me. Your prayers help enable me to hear from God clearly.

# INTRODUCTION

## BECOMING AN EXTRAORDINARY LEADER
### Impacting Others to Lead

Whether being called to lead a world-wide ministry, a local church, or a ten-person cell group, there is far more to being called into a position of leadership in the Body of Christ than meets the eye. The Lord is raising up a new breed of extraordinary leaders, including you and I, who are willing to walk in "impact leadership."

The dictionary gives us several definitions for the word "impact." One refers to the impression made by a person, thing, or idea. Another refers to the force or impetus caused by a collision. As called leaders in the Body of Christ, it is our job to not only leave an indelible impression on those we lead, but to be willing to collide "head-on" with the lethargy and apathy found too often in society, and even in church leadership, in order to equip others for the end-time harvest.

The need for us to rise up as extraordinary leaders who are willing to not only make an impact, but impact others to lead, is all too clear.

While being driven to the airport after a recent three-day ministry engagement, the driver confided that she had learned more and been offered more of an opportunity to use her gifts in those three days than she had in her home church in the previous three or four months.

In another instance, at the end of my first session out of five on "Ministering in the Gifts," a woman ran up to me, bursting with excitement, saying, "This has been so good! I felt a confidence rise up in me and fear lift off of me." She continued, "It is rare to find a minister willing to teach, train, and activate the gifts God has placed in you. They usually only talk about it."

What a sad commentary these examples are on the state of church leadership. And these are just two of many such incidences and comments.

As today's leaders, whether veteran pastors over large churches or newly appointed facilitators of small home cell groups, it is up to us to effect a change. It is up to us to answer God's call and become true impact leaders.

God is placing an "Apostolic" call on His church leadership today, a call to multiply the spread of the Gospel by becoming a "training, equipping and sending" mechanism for the end times. He is sounding a recall for the church to return to the "laying on of hands" reproduction and sending out of leadership, such as we witness in the book of Acts, 2 Timothy, and throughout the New Testament.

*"Now in the church (assembly) at Antioch there were prophets (inspired interpreters of the will and purposes of God) and teachers: Barnabas, Symeon who was called Niger (black) Lucius of Cyrene, Manaen a member of the court of Herod the Tetrarch, and Saul. While they were worshipping the Lord and fasting, the Holy Spirit said, separate now for me Barnabas and Saul for the work to which I have called them. Then after fasting and praying, they put their hands on them and sent them away."* Acts 13:1-3

*"For this reason I remind you to fan into flame the gift of God, which is in you through the laying on of my hands."* 2 Timothy 1:6

During my travels in ministry, I am repeatedly hearing the sound of church members crying out for the training they so desperately need to enable them to effectively use the gifts of the Holy Spirit in order to reach and impact those who are lost, sick and dying. God is placing a hunger in His people to desire more of His anointing to be imparted through leadership.

*Then He said to His disciples, "The harvest is plentiful, but the workers are few. Therefore beseech the Lord of the harvest to send out workers into the harvest." Matthew 9:37-38*

Jesus Christ ministered to the multitudes, yet He spent valuable time with His disciples whom He trained to become apostles.  He is our example. It is this same reproduction phenomenon that will launch us, today, on the path of preparation for the end-time harvest.

That is why I'm writing this book.  The Lord has moved on me to help my co-laborers, especially those just launching into leadership, to understand the fullness of what is involved in impact leadership, from the reasons it is needed to the practical ways to put it into effect in our ministries.

Together, we must determine to move beyond the ordinary, become conditioned, and ready ourselves as extraordinary leaders, then purpose to raise up other leaders who not only have impact themselves, but are able to impact others and reproduce yet more well-equipped leaders.

# Table of Contents

## BECOMING AN EXTRAORDINARY LEADER
## Impacting Others to Lead

| | |
|---|---|
| Endorsements | iii |
| Acknowledgements | v |
| Introduction | vii |
| Forward | xiii |

**SEC. I – BECOMING AN EXTRAORDINARY LEADER**

| | |
|---|---|
| Chapter 1 – God's View of Leadership | 3 |
| Chapter 2 – Grasping the Vision | 9 |
| Chapter 3 – Conquering Fear | 13 |
| Chapter 4 – The Call to Humility | 19 |
| Chapter 5 – Guarding Your Heart | 25 |
| Chapter 6 – Accentuating the Positive | 33 |
| Chapter 7 – Leading From Your Knees | 39 |
| Chapter 8 – Answering the Apostolic Call | 43 |

**SEC. II – IMPACTING OTHERS TO LEAD**

| | |
|---|---|
| Chapter 9 – Modeling Respect for Authority | 49 |
| Chapter 10 – Leading by Example | 55 |
| Chapter 11 – Flowing in the Believer's Anointing | 59 |
| Chapter 12 – Reproducing & Releasing Leaders | 67 |
| Chapter 13 – Nurturing & Using God's Gifts | 77 |
| Chapter 14 – Impacting Children & Youth | 83 |
| Chapter 15 – Initiating Change and Embracing the New | 85 |
| Chapter 16 – Walking Together in Membership Ministry | 93 |
| Heart to Heart | xv |
| About the Author | xvii |
| About Jimmie Reed Ministries | xix |
| About the Editor | xxiii |
| Other Available Ministry Tools | xxv |

# FORWARD TO

## BECOMING AN EXTRAORDINARY LEADER
### By
### Dr. Jimmie Reed

It has always been my premise that leaders are made, not born. Of course, natural gifting and a fire in the belly are always helpful in the development of extraordinary leaders for God's Kingdom. But truly, leaders are to be developed, and is one of the primary responsibilities of all spiritual leaders today.

The development of leaders for the local church and beyond requires a thorough understanding of the principles of leadership. Further, it is essential for today's leaders to have a vision that takes them beyond the building of ministry for this generation alone. A view to the future, to spiritual children and grand children is needed, along with skilled sensitive mentoring of the present and future generations.

Many of the principles needed to accomplish this task are clearly and passionately presented in Dr. Jimmie Reed's dynamic book, *Becoming an Extraordinary Leader*. It is filled with keen insights, rooted in the word of God with practical wisdom for leaders and those in leadership training. Key in training a potential leader is the development of Christian character to under gird the gifts of the individual being trained. Dr. Reed focuses much of her writing on the issue of character, something desperately needed in leadership training today.

As a prophetic leader herself, Jimmie Reed knows from which she speaks. Having gone through the trials often accompanying leadership, she presents her principles with a real world context. The practical wisdom found in the pages of this book will be a blessing to students and seasoned leaders alike.

Dr. Stan DeKoven
President
Vision International University

Section 1

# BECOMING AN EXTRAORDINARY LEADER

# Chapter 1
# GOD'S VIEW OF LEADERSHIP

There are callings (like those listed in Mark 16:17-18), that are common to all that believe, and all of God's people are called to the ministry of reconciliation (2 Cor. 5:18), and prayer (1 Thess. 5:17). But not every believer is called to leadership.

Since you are reading this book, you are likely operating in, or believe you are called to be operating in, a position of leadership. The key question is, are you or will you be leading in a manner that has true impact for the Lord, both on those you minister to and those you will raise up in leadership alongside you?

**What Is a Leader?**

There is leadership in every facet of society. Gangs have leaders, terrorist bands have leaders, corporations have leaders, civic organizations and governments have leaders.

But don't make the mistake of confusing the attributes of leaders in the world with the qualities of true impact leaders in the body of Christ.

Some common dictionary definitions of the word "leader" include: "One who leads; a person of commanding authority and influence;" "Someone who acts as a guide, a directing head or chief;" or "Someone who leads a body of moving troops." While these definitions can also apply to Christian leadership, they stop short of God's biblical definition of leadership.

As is so often the case, the world's definition of a leader varies somewhat from God's definition.

In the body of Christ leaders can come in one of three categories: those who are self-appointed, those who are hirelings and those who are called and gifted by God for positions of leadership.

**Self-Appointed Leaders**

When we allow our carnal mind (which, according to Romans 8:7, is at enmity with God) to rule us, our ego can decide for us that we would like to be in a position of leadership. After all, those in leadership have power, are generally respected, well compensated, treated with dignity, etc., and these are all things our human nature craves. For worldly leadership this may work, but to be a spiritual leader it is necessary to allow the spirit, not the carnal ego and natural cravings, to be in control.

The Word clearly shows us that it is not to be us, but God, who prepares us for leadership and promotes us through His wisdom and sovereignty. He expects us, as His children, to let Him decide our position, and even warns us repeatedly against self-promotion:

*"Wisdom is the principal thing; therefore get wisdom: and with all thy getting get understanding. Exalt her, and she shall promote thee: she shall bring thee to honour, when thou dost embrace her."* (Prov. 4:7-8)

*"For promotion cometh neither from the east, nor from the west, nor from the south. But God is the judge: he putteth down one, and setteth up another."* (Psa. 75:6-7)

*"For I say, through the grace given unto me, to every man that is among you, not to think of himself more highly than he ought to think; but to think soberly, according as God hath dealt to every man the measure of faith."* (Rom. 12:3)

*"Let every man abide in the same calling wherein he was called."* (1 Cor. 7:20)

The biggest danger of someone trying to appoint oneself to leadership in the body of Christ is that such a leader will be on his/her own. God has promised to supply everything you need to do what He has called you to do, but He is not obligated to provide for those who choose to "do it themselves," instead of following in His will. Of all people, those who would be leaders in the body of Christ need to realize that they are "bought with a price" and only glorify God when they are doing His will, not their own.

## The Ineffectiveness of the Hireling

Some have made the mistake of becoming pastors or ministry leaders because it is considered as a good, secure, and decent occupation. These misguided folks may be saved and love the Lord, but have not taken the time and effort to seek Him as to what He wants them to do with their lives. Instead they make a practical career decision.

Jesus makes clear the distinction between a called "shepherd," or leader, who is devoted to doing whatever the Lord leads him/her to do to reach, love and care for His people, and a "hireling" who simply takes a stable job working in church leadership:

*"I am the good shepherd: the good shepherd giveth his life for the sheep. But he that is an hireling, and not the shepherd, whose own the sheep are not, seeth the wolf coming, and leaveth the sheep, and fleeth: and the wolf catcheth them, and scattereth the sheep. The hireling fleeth, because he is an hireling, and careth not for the sheep."* (John 10:11-13)

Not only is the hireling not shepherding or leading like Jesus, but he/she can actually be putting the flock they are leading in jeopardy, because they lack the love and devotion it takes to lead wisely and safely, protecting the flock from danger.

## Called and Anointed As a Leader

That love and devotion for the flock is a part of the gifting God provides when He calls a man or woman to become a "shepherd," or leader. When you are truly called and anointed of God for leadership, and you submit to that call,

He will enable you to become humble and self-sacrificing – truly able to "lay down your life," i.e., your own personal ambitions and dreams – so you can fulfill His desires instead.

When you know you have been called by God into a leadership position in the body of Christ it should be taken seriously. It is indeed a privilege to be called to the "holy" calling of leadership, but not one that we can take any credit for ourselves. God chose you not because of how worthy you are, but simply because it is part of His bigger plan:

*"Who hath saved us, and called us with an holy calling, not according to our works, but according to his own purpose and grace, which was given us in Christ Jesus before the world began."* (2 Tim. 1:9)

**A Higher Standard**

Being called to Christian leadership by God means being called to a higher standard of lifestyle and behavior than is needed to be in leadership in the world.

If you look at Paul's "job descriptions" for leadership (see 1 Tim. 3:2-3) where he discusses bishops and deacons, you'll see listed the character traits and behavior patterns still necessary for a good church leader today:

- Blameless
- Faithful – not a philanderer
- Apt to teach
- Not abusive
- Not greedy
- Patient
- Not covetous
- In control of his/her household
- Not immature
- Not hypocritical

**A LEADER IS NOT EXPECTED TO BE PERFECT,** but anyone not willing to try to live up to these criteria should not consider themselves, nor be considered, a true leader in the body of Christ.

**MANY ARE CALLED, FEW ARE CHOSEN.**

It's not that you might not be called as a leader, but you must be willing to work at allowing God to make you "worthy of your calling." Then, as a good leader, you should also pray for that, as Paul did, for those you lead (see 2 Thess. 1:11-12).

If you feel you are called as a leader, but have not yet been made "worthy of your calling," don't despair.

Even if you have been backslidden, or are leading a hypocritical "double-minded" lifestyle trying to walk the fence between God and the world, your call is just waiting for you to repent and submit yourself and begin to fulfill it.

God has not changed His mind, nor His plan for you, because you have not yet become spiritually equipped for His kind of leadership.

*"For the gifts and calling of God are without repentance."* (Rom. 11:29)

God will not change His mind. Once He has called you to spiritual leadership, the call is always there, waiting for you to submit to whatever preparation may still be necessary so that you can walk in it.

Jesus was more than a "good example". Through His leadership and through His obedience to fulfill His calling, He made an everlasting impact on the world. We live in a world today where the things of God are no longer respected and taken for granted as they were in societies past.

As God's leaders today we too need to become more than just decent examples. We need to become extraordinary, to create an impact on those we lead, on society, and on the church.

# Becoming an Extraordinary Leader

The dictionary gives us several definitions for the word "impact." One refers to the impression made by a person, thing, or idea. Another refers to the force or impetus caused by a collision.

## Leaving an Impression

As called leaders in the body of Christ, it is our job to not only leave an indelible impression on those we lead, but to be willing to collide "head-on" with the lethargy and apathy found too often in society and even in church leadership.

To be an extraordinary leader, like Jesus, we must think differently than the average person, even differently than some leaders. We must have a clear vision of the assignment the Lord has given us to fulfill. We must realize that if we take our eyes off the goal we will begin to see the obstacles all around us, so instead we press in.

We must see obstacles as an opportunity for growth, stay goal focused and, instead of giving up, must work at removing limitations and overcoming barriers.

## Assigned to Impact

As chosen spiritual leaders we have an assignment, a goal, to become leaders who make an impact, like Jesus, and to equip others for the end-time harvest. We must press in fearlessly, yet filled with humility, knowing the powerful, almighty God we serve.

We must teach with authority, lead by example, and reproduce ourselves. We must be willing to sometimes put aside past ways of leadership, whether effective or ineffective, and embrace new ideas as God leads us (see Isaiah 43:19). We must be initiators of change and learn to walk together with other believers and leaders, recognizing and utilizing all of God's gifts.

This is God's view of leadership, and if we are to become extraordinary leaders, like Jesus, we must hold His standard.

## Chapter 2
## GRASPING THE VISION

You can't be a leader without a vision.

No matter how anointed you are, no matter how much you love the Lord and want to serve Him, you cannot be an extraordinary leader, a leader who will make a true impact, without a God-given vision for the work He has called you to do.

Every believer should be seeking God for a personal vision for their purpose, their destiny – a goal to be working toward accomplishing with their lives. And God will reveal it, often one step at a time, as we spend time with Him and open ourselves to His leading.

But when you believe God has called you to a position of leadership, whether over a home cell group or a ministry reaching the multitudes, the first thing you must do is seek Him for a vision for the people He has given you to lead and to reach and for the work He has ordained you to lead them to fulfill.

**Having a Sure Vision**

As I lead those the Lord puts before me, one piece of exhortation I often quote is: "If you don't know where you're going, any road will take you there."

Just knowing you are called to leadership is not enough to immediately start a work, or plunge into leadership. Sometimes a person's zealousness for becoming a leader will cause them to move ahead of God, to their own sorrow and perhaps the detriment of others.

The Word warns us of the importance of having a sure vision:

*"Where there is no vision, the people perish".* (Prov. 29:18a)

## Seek God for the Vision

The first step in leadership is to seek God for the vision. As we are diligent to do this, God will reveal the purpose of your leadership call and give you a solid vision you can put before others so they will be willing to follow you as you accomplish it:

*"And the LORD answered me, and said, Write the vision, and make it plain upon tables, that he may run that readeth it. For the vision is yet for an appointed time, but at the end it shall speak, and not lie: though it tarry, wait for it; because it will surely come, it will not tarry."* (Hab. 2:2-3)

Notice that God not only wanted Habbukuk to write the vision in a way that would be clear to those who would run with him to perform it, but He reminded him that the timing of the fulfillment of the vision was up to Him, and even if it seemed delayed it was a sure thing.

## It's Your Move!

As God plants the vision in our hearts, it is up to us to do something with it.

I see it rather like a Divine chess game. God is the Chief Player. He makes the first move by calling us to leadership. We make the next move as we seek Him for the vision.

God gives us the vision. Our move is to accept it and ask for instruction. He gives the instruction and opportunity, and it is our move to obey and help Him to bring it to pass. We make our calling and election sure (2 Peter 1:10).

He doesn't make any more moves until we make our move in response to His move. We truly become co-laborers with Him to bring His vision to pass (1 Cor. 3:9).

## Sharing the Vision

One thing that separates leaders from the flock is that they see the whole corporate vision God has given. But a leader is, by definition, not expected to move or accomplish the vision alone. A leader shares the glory and excitement of their God-given vision with others, who then will come alongside them and work with them to see the vision fulfilled.

As you solidify and share the vision for your calling, God will move on the hearts of others and reveal His greater purpose. Then others will be willing to bring their personal vision in under the greater vision.

For example, God gave David a vision for leading His people and becoming King. Jonathan's destiny, on the other hand, was to receive the throne of Kingship by inheritance from his father Saul. However, when God gave Jonathan a larger view, and revealed a greater purpose for David to come into that inheritance, Jonathan chose to covenant with his friend David and flow with him for God's greater purpose.

As you grasp the vision God has given you as a called leader in the body of Christ, it is your part to seek Him, purpose to grow in His character, share the vision with others, and once they get the vision inside of them, raise them up to labor with you.

An extraordinary leader will seek for clarity of vision, strategize to fulfill the vision, appoint those around them for different aspects of the vision, and then walk alongside of them, activating them in their gifts, to see the completion of the vision.

## Chapter 3
## CONQUERING FEAR

Often preparing to step out in obedience to God's call and vision for your life can be overwhelming to the flesh. To do and be all God has called you, you must learn to conquer your fears and put your total trust in Him.

This can't be done in our flesh, but we can walk in the Spirit!

Fear can attack even God's choicest servants. It may come for varying reasons and in varying ways.

Consider the Biblical account of Jesus calming the storm, found in Mark 4.

*"And he said unto them, Why are ye so fearful? How is it that ye have no faith? And they feared exceedingly, and said one to another, What manner of man is this, that even the wind and the sea obey him?"* (Mark 4:40-41)

Even though these were His potential key leaders, they were "exceedingly" afraid because they did not yet truly understand who Jesus was, and what He would do for them.

**The Need to Know Him**

Often, until we truly get into a close personal relationship with Jesus, and become confident of His call on our life, we don't know Him well enough to know that we needn't be afraid of the storms surrounding us, nor do we need be afraid of Him and what He is about to do.

One of the best ways to be prepared to conquer fear is to get into a deep relationship with Him, through His Word and prayer, and build confidence that the same Spirit that raised Him from the dead dwells big in you.

Because God's visions are always so much bigger than anything we are capable of doing in the natural, even the most stalwart believer can sometimes find an ungodly spirit of fear creeping in, trying to make them doubt the vision, or at least their ability to help bring it to pass.

Perhaps the scope and reality of the assignment you recognize God is giving you has caused you to allow fear and doubt to come into your mind.

We must continually remind ourselves that it is not God that gives us a spirit of fear or intimidation (2 Tim. 1:7). Fear is not a fruit of the Spirit, but peace is.

If we have had fear over the fulfillment of destiny, we need to come to a place of peace with the vision God has given us. This will take dying to our carnal nature, and walking in the Spirit.

But what if you know you've been called to be one of God's extraordinary leaders, called with a momentous vision, and you have let fear or doubt slip in?

Will your fear or reticence to step out as He calls you to be a leader and fulfill His vision stop God's plan? I think not. His Word says that "the gifts and callings of God are without repentance," (Rom. 11:29) meaning He doesn't change His mind.

## No Condemnation

We must not let condemnation come in if we have, momentarily, allowed fear to deter us from moving forward as an impact leader. There is no condemnation to them who are in Christ Jesus! (See Rom. 8)

So what does happen when someone has been given specific instructions from God and is feeling afraid to step out and obey? Take a moment to read Joshua 1:1-11.

Notice that God gave Joshua encouragement and specific instructions as to how to take over leadership after Moses died. This was a big assignment, so God did not just bark a quick order and leave Joshua hanging with his mouth open in amazement. Our God is much too loving, and too thorough, for that.

Note the care with which He handled Joshua, and the encouragement and moral support He offered. Don't you know you can trust Him to do the same for you?

Not only did He remind him of the importance of knowing His Word, but of being bold and strong, not letting his fear stop him.

*"Have not I commanded thee? Be strong and of a good courage; be not afraid, neither be thou dismayed: for the LORD thy God is with thee whithersoever thou goest."* (Joshua 1:9)

We know God doesn't waste either His time or His words, so we must assume that if He told Joshua to "be not afraid" it was because, knowing Joshua's heart, He knew there was fear trying to slow him down or stop him from doing what God had commanded him to do.

But instead of being put off by Joshua's potential fear, God gave Him the reassurance he needed to put aside the fear and step out in obedience. The rest, as they say, is history.

**Fear of Failure**

One of the primary fears that will try to rear its ugly head when we have been given a vision from God is fear of failure. We look at how big the vision seems and suddenly we see ourselves as totally inadequate.

Some of the scouts sent to check out the promised land fell victim to this kind of fear. Instead of focusing, as Joshua and Caleb did, on the surety of God's promise, they looked at the potential obstacles and became "as grasshoppers in their own eyes." (Num. 13:33)

Were they inadequate? Not with God's promises behind them. But their refusal to trust God and His promise kept them from being a part of the glorious fulfillment of the vision of the land promised to God's people. They let fear rob them of their destiny.

## Failure Is Totally Unnecessary

The most important thing to realize when we think of their failure is that it was totally unnecessary. Had they taken their eyes off of the natural circumstances and kept their eyes on the God that had been proving Himself to them all their lives, their outcome would have been totally different.

So the most important lesson learned from their experience is to keep your focus on God and His promise. If He has given you a vision to fulfill for Him, it is His responsibility to bring it to pass if you simply trust and obey.

Step forth under His almighty authority, lead those under you through His delegated authority, and you needn't fear failure.

No matter what it might look like to our natural senses, it's a sure victory! We can all fail, in the flesh, but our God can't fail!

## Fear of Losing Your Authority

Another lie of the enemy that may try to plague you when you begin to set forth in the vision God has given you is that of losing your authority, which is your power to accomplish it for Him.

It is inevitable that there will be others, who either don't know the Lord or are very immature in their relationship with Him, who are jealous of the gifts and the vision God has given you. Some will even try to usurp your authority, steal or duplicate your vision, and attempt to "take credit" for what is being done.

Like any spirit of fear, this too is groundless. We need to remind ourselves that God has had an individual plan for each of our lives since before the foundation of the world. God already planned for you to be the one to fulfill the vision He has for your ministry, and no one can stop it but you.

Make this your proclamation of victory:

*"The LORD is on my side; I will not fear: what can man do unto me?"* (Psa. 118:6)

Because God gave us our free will we can always refuse to fulfill our destiny and complete the vision He has for our lives and ministry. But, barring that, God will not be stopped!

## Keep Stepping Forward

Others may try to undermine, they may try to take over, they may betray you, they may try to put stumblingblocks in your path. But if you "know that you know," deep in your heart, that God has given you this calling, this vision, this destiny, then all you have to do is keep stepping toward it.

Of course you must always be mindful to listen to the Holy Spirit, so you will know when to stand still, when to move forward, when to share ideas and visions and when to hold your peace.

Don't panic if it seems that someone is trying to overtake your vision. If you can't be used to help them get back on the right track and work toward their own vision, then just keep moving and leave them to God.

If you get pulled into the flesh and become fearful or doubtful, it may leave room for the enemy to use someone or something to short-circuit what God is doing for a season. But if you repent of being misled into the flesh, come back to Him and commit to continuing toward the goal, He will put you right back on track.

## Nothing Is Impossible With Him

Even if you have been so pulled off your vision that it seems impossible, you must remember that with God nothing is impossible!

Your vision is definitely bigger than you are. It is definitely something you, in yourself, cannot bring to pass. But you needn't fear failure, nor fear someone robbing you of your vision, because you can be confident that God is faithful, God is just, and God is determined to complete what He starts.

*"Being confident of this very thing, that he which hath begun a good work in you will perform it until the day of Jesus Christ."* (Phil. 1:6)

## Chapter 4
## THE CALL TO HUMILITY

It is essential for someone who is called to leadership to develop the Godly characteristics necessary to be an extraordinary leader, one who will truly make a difference in the sphere God has called him or her to influence.

While pride and self-confidence may be the attributes most valued in a worldly leader, the Biblical definition is the opposite. Humility, meekness, and servitude are the attributes the Scriptures say show true leadership.

A call to leadership is truly a call to humilty:

*"But he that is greatest among you shall be your servant. And whosoever shall exalt himself shall be abased; and he that shall humble himself shall be exalted."* (Matt. 23:11-12)

Some definitions of "humble" are: not proud, haughty, arrogant or assertive; reflecting, expressing, or offered in a spirit of deference or submission. As a verb, to "humble" is to make humble in spirit or manner; to destroy the power, independence or prestige of.

Humility before the Lord destroys our independence and our reliance on ourselves, and puts us in a position to truly be dependent on His Spirit.

It is only when we position ourselves His way that He can lift us up and exalt us to a position of true impact leadership.

*"...Yea, all of you be subject one to another, and be clothed with humility: for God resisteth the proud, and giveth grace to the humble. Humble yourselves therefore under the mighty hand of God, that he may exalt you in due time."* (1 Peter 5:5b-6)

One synonym for humility is meekness. Dictionary definitions of the word "meek" include: endures injury with patience; submissive, non-violent.

Many in the world would not consider that a valid description of a true leader, yet Jesus refers to Himself as both meek and lowly (see Matt. 11:29). If there was ever anyone who has walked on earth who submitted to His divine assignment, endured injury with patience, and manifested non-violence it was our Lord.

**Walking in the Spirit**

Humility is an attribute free from pride and the Word indicates it is attainable by God's saints. So, if we are to be extraordinary leaders we must not only preach humility, but demonstrate it by our own personal walk.

The catch is that no matter how much we want to be obedient, especially as leaders, it is impossible for us be truly meek and humble in our flesh. Our flesh is being run by a carnal mind that is at enmity with God (see Romans 8:7), full of pride, ego, and impatience.

Thankfully, it is possible for us to walk humbly before our Lord by submitting our flesh to the dominion and authority of the Holy Spirit, as the Apostle Paul reminds us:

*"This I say then, Walk in the Spirit, and ye shall not fulfil the lust of the flesh."* (Gal 5:16)

This will allow us to put away our desire for personal glory and use our leadership impact to glorify God:

*"If we live in the Spirit, let us also walk in the Spirit. Let us not be desirous of vain glory, provoking one another, envying one another."* (Gal. 5:25–26)

Once we have truly humbled ourselves before God, determined to walk in the Spirit and launched into our calling as extraordinary leaders, humility will become an integral part of our leadership.

## The Call to Humility

### Humbling Ourselves Before Others

The Bible even admonishes us, in Galatians 6:1-3, that when we are ministering to others, it must be done in a spirit of meekness, not thinking of ourselves as being important, but stressing their necessity for the leading of the Holy Spirit and God's Word.

Jesus was willing to minister to those under His leadership to the point of humbling Himself to wash the disciples' feet, even though He is the King of Kings and Lord of Lords.

He advised us to be willing to "turn the other cheek" when under attack (see Matthew 5:38), a true act of humbling yourself before another.

And, although it goes against all the "me first," "survival mentality" and "self-protection" credos of the world, as followers of Jesus we must put others first:

*"Be kindly affectioned one to another with brotherly love; in honour preferring one another."* (Rom. 12:10)

And these commandments don't lessen when we become leaders, but in fact become even more important. It is becoming wise and working to fulfill your calling while maintaining Godly humility that will bring the blessings and favor of God on your life and ministry.

*"The king's favour is toward a wise servant, but his wrath is against him that causeth shame."* (Prov. 14:35)

### Deliverance Through Humility

Humbling ourselves before others, particularly those in leadership over us, can allow God to lead us into deliverance.

One of my potential leaders came into my office looking troubled one day, saying he just wanted a talk with his pastor. Finally he opened his heart: "I've been asked to consider going back through inner healing and deliverance," he said, "but I've already been through it and God did a lot of work in my life."

He went on to explain that he had grown up with abuse, and had been very angry. Even though he had been determined not to carry on the abuse, those same abusive traits he'd seen in his family had begun to manifest in him.

Once he realized what he was seeing, he went through deliverance and God took away the spirit of anger and abuse.

But I sensed there was a current problem, so I asked, "What's going on now?"

Looking sheepish he confessed, "Well, I know God has delivered me, but now someone has told me I need to go through deliverance because of fear."

**Another Layer of Deliverance**

When we discussed the issue of fear and he began to mention some more recent situations in his life, I agreed that it was indeed time for him to go through another layer of deliverance and inner healing.

I explained that while the first deliverance had made him free from anger and abuse, the Lord now wanted to do additional deliverance in the area of fear so that He could take him to another level.

This man of God had been willing to humble himself to speak with me, as his pastor, about a potential problem. He then humbled himself to allow the Lord to take him through additional healing and deliverance.

Because of his humility, this saint has now been delivered of fear, is freer in all aspects of his life and able to serve in the church in a wonderful capacity.

This example shows how humility can make the difference between being stagnated and defeated and being able to grow into leadership potential. We must never let natural or spiritual pride stop us from receiving God's deliverance.

Once at a leadership workshop, I was asked, "How do you keep potential leaders motivated? Is it wise to teach others what you know?"

## The Call to Humility

### Humility Gives Freely

My reply was this, "A true impact leader who desires to walk in humility will want to see others come up to higher levels even than themselves. In motivating others to new levels, they also are increased and God can begin to compel them and open doors for them to go into greater levels of ministry than ever before."

She responded, "How do you walk in humility?" It is a worthwhile question. One of the ways is to allow God to transform your heart so that it is lacking the kind of pride that says "I always need to be in the forefront. I need to always be the one who is seen."

We need to be reminded that Jesus Christ raised His disciples up into greater measures. Pride hangs on tightly to what it has, but humility gives freely.

The person who had raised the original question began to see how humility plays a great role in motivating us as impact leaders to become those who motivate others into leadership.

### Laying Down Our Lives

But true humility goes even beyond humbling ourselves and giving freely of ourselves to motivate others.

The example Jesus set for us is that of a "Good Shepherd". Jesus described the extraordinary leadership of true shepherds, as opposed to the worldly leadership of a hireling, by their willingness to lay down their lives for those whom they are called to lead.

*"I am the good shepherd, and know my sheep, and am known of mine. As the Father knoweth me, even so know I the Father: and I lay down my life for the sheep."* (John 10:14 )

*"This is my commandment, That ye love one another, as I have loved you. Greater love hath no man than this, that a man lay down his life for his friends."* (John 15:12-15)

*"Hereby perceive we the love of God, because he laid down his life for us: and we ought to lay down our lives for the brethren."* (1John 3:16)

Our Christ-like willingness to lay down our lives for those we lead is the ultimate expression of humility and love.

## Chapter 5
## GUARDING YOUR HEART

Another characteristic of Jesus that we must develop, in order to be a truly extraordinary leader, is a heart after God's own heart. You must have a heart of love, compassion, forgiveness and joy – a heart of praise, worship, repentance and obedience. A pure heart.

That may sound like a tall order, but remember there is nothing impossible with God.

Does having that kind of heart mean you will have to be perfect? Hardly.

As mighty a man of God as King David turned out to be, he was by no means perfect. He sinned more than once – numbering the people when God told him not to, lusting after another man's wife, having a man killed in order to take his wife as his own, etc. – but yet we are told that God testified to David being a man after His own heart (see Acts 13:22).

How can that be? It is because when God looks at His called and anointed servants He is not looking from our earthly perspective. He is a God who is looking past the extraneous things and directly into the heart.

**A Heart to Fulfill ALL His Will**

God could look past David's sinful actions and straight to his heart, just as He looked past his physical appearance and straight to his heart when He sent Samuel to anoint David. David had a compassionate heart, a heart of praise and worship for God, and a repentant heart.

But, even more importantly, David had an obedient heart. In that same verse in Acts where it says God called David a man after His own heart, it goes on to say "which shall fulfill all My will."

While love, compassion, forgiveness, joy and repentance are all key factors in having a heart after God, the primary ingredient is obedience.

God needs leaders for His body today who are willing to do "all His will" if His purposes are going to be fulfilled. That requires a pure heart, a heart of absolute obedience.

After all, what good does it do the purposes of God if someone's heart is compassionate, joyful, loving, and even repentant, if they are not ultimately going to accomplish what He has called them to do?

**Our Deceitful Heart**

How, you may ask yourself, can I have a pure and obedient heart, when the Word itself tells me (see Jer. 17:9) that our hearts are, by nature, deceitful and more desperately wicked than even we can realize?

The answer is simple. You can't.

But that's perfectly okay, because none of us can do anything worthwhile of ourselves. Without Him we can do nothing, remember? (see John 15:5)

**Preparing Your Heart**

When we determine, as servants of God, to fulfill His call on our lives and His vision for our ministries, we must also determine to die to our flesh and let His Holy Spirit take over – beginning with our hearts (which are deceitful and wicked) and our minds (which are at enmity with God).

The importance of preparing our hearts can mean the difference between Godly leadership and evil leadership, as can be clearly seen in the scriptural account of King Rehoboam:

*"And he did evil, because he prepared not his heart to seek the LORD."* (2 Chron. 12:14)

So an important factor in being prepared for impact leadership, and being able to continue leading with impact, is to prepare our hearts. Since this is not something we can do for ourselves, we must submit our hearts to the Lord and allow His Holy Spirit to teach us:

*"Teach me thy way, O LORD; I will walk in thy truth: unite my heart to fear thy name. I will praise thee, O Lord my God, with all my heart: and I will glorify thy name for evermore."* (Psa. 86:11-12)

David understood that, in himself, he could not fulfill his call. His cry before God was that He would take his wicked heart and clean it up, acknowledging that only when it was under the rule of the Holy Spirit could he begin to teach God's truth and see sinners saved:

*"Create in me a clean heart, O God; and renew a right spirit within me. Cast me not away from thy presence; and take not thy holy spirit from me. Restore unto me the joy of thy salvation; and uphold me with thy free spirit. Then will I teach transgressors thy ways; and sinners shall be converted unto thee."* (Psa. 51:10-13)

**Draw Near With a True Heart**

We can never be true leaders without staying in very close relationship with the Lord. The Apostle Paul acknowledged that the only way we could draw near to God with a true heart was by allowing the Holy Spirit and the Word to cleanse us:

*"Let us draw near with a true heart in full assurance of faith, having our hearts sprinkled from an evil conscience, and our bodies washed with pure water."* (Heb. 10:22)

**Let Him Do the Work**

Even if we have prepared our heart and are determined to guard it, there will be times when the circumstances around us will push us back into the flesh.

When I was going through a season of very difficult, very challenging, circumstances I recognized my heart was not in the place it needed to be.

I asked Him to renew a right spirit within me, and remembering the prayer of David in Psalms 51 was a lifeline for me.

It was through praying this prayer for myself that God was able to show me the weaknesses in me that He wanted to mend, and once I had submitted them to Him He even began to give me discernment into the heart motives of others.

Be patient with yourself as you progress through the sometimes painful preparation for a pure heart. God is willing to dig through the layers of heart issues that have been holding us back to get us to the place where we can be healed, free and ready to press on to the greater things with a pure heart.

**Guarding Your Heart**

Once we have submitted to the Lord and presented our hearts to Him to purify, it doesn't end there. We are responsible for guarding our heart and keeping it pure.

*"Keep [guard] thy heart with all diligence; for out of it are the issues of life."* (Prov. 4:23)

Our carnal nature is constantly pulling on us with temptations and fleshly desires in order to pull us away from God, particularly after we have acknowledged His call on our life to leadership. The Bible says that it is from the heart that all issues of life flow. That means that whoever rules our heart, rules all the issues of our life.

If we let our flesh, or the enemy, keep authority over our heart, then we cannot walk in the Spirit.

The verse (Prov. 4:23) referenced guarding our heart "with all diligence." That means there is some effort, some work involved. We cannot take having a pure heart for granted. It is something we must continually work at, by continually keeping ourselves pulled out of the flesh and into the spirit.

When we allow the Lord to take over He will continually enlarge our hearts with His love, compassion, joy, praise, repentance and obedience, so that we can continue running for Him until the end:

*"I will run the way of thy commandments, when thou shalt enlarge my heart. Teach me, O LORD, the way of thy statutes; and I shall keep it unto the end."* (Psa. 119:32-33)

## Expecting & Overcoming Attacks

As leaders we are subjected to great onslaughts of the enemy through both circumstances and people. It is to be expected.

Jesus said (in John 15) that they will hate us, just as they did Him, and they will persecute us, just as they did Him.

Since the beginning, those who have been called by God as leaders have suffered persecution, unfair attacks, and bitter campaigns of lies.

As these challenging events come up in your ministry walk, if you have your heart fixed and steadfastly submitted to the Holy Spirit, you can be in agreement with David and keep moving forward in praise and victory in spite of the obstacles:

*"They have prepared a net for my steps; my soul is bowed down: they have digged a pit before me, into the midst whereof they are fallen themselves. My heart is fixed, O God, my heart is fixed: I will sing and give praise."* (Psa. 57:6-7)

If we are to be extraordinary leaders who will make great impact, we must rise above our natural tendency to panic at setbacks, whine over offenses, and become bitter over lies and betrayals, and respond with the emotions of the Holy Spirit instead – love, joy, peace, long-suffering (patience), gentleness, goodness, faith, meekness and temperance.

## Benefits of a Pure Heart

One of the benefits of guarding our heart and keeping it pure is that it is then that the Lord will hear and answer our prayers:

*"If I regard iniquity in my heart, the Lord will not hear me."* (Psa. 66:18)

As an impact leader it is important that the words we speak always glorify God and draw others to Him. When our hearts are submitted to Jesus, we can be a "good man," able to bring forth good with our speech:

*"A good man out of the good treasure of his heart bringeth forth that which is good; and an evil man out of the evil treasure of his heart bringeth forth that which is evil: for of the abundance of the heart his mouth speaketh."* (Luke 6:45)

Allowing the Holy Spirit to cleanse your heart will keep you able to walk in the love necessary to truly impact those you are leading:

*"Seeing ye have purified your souls in obeying the truth through the Spirit unto unfeigned love of the brethren, see that ye love one another with a pure heart fervently."* (1 Peter 1:22)

A pure heart, submitted to the leading of the Holy Spirit, is never going to be double-minded. Instead it can be fixed and steadfast. This will give true leaders the peace and courage needed to step out boldly to do all God has called them to do.

If we can keep our heart fixed and obedient, we don't need to fear bad news:

*"He shall not be afraid of evil tidings: his heart is fixed, trusting in the LORD."* (Psa. 112:7)

When our heart is pure, and fixed on Jesus, we will have the peace that is promised and be able to keep our thoughts full of what is good around us, not what is evil:

*"And the peace of God, which passeth all understanding, shall keep your hearts and minds through Christ Jesus. Finally, brethren, whatsoever things are true, whatsoever things are honest, whatsoever things are just, whatsoever things are pure, whatsoever things are*

*lovely, whatsoever things are of good report; if there be any virtue, and if there be any praise, think on these things."* (Phil. 4:7-8)

Do you want to be able to walk a pure, holy, compassionate, repentant and obedient walk and be the best example you possibly can be of Jesus to those you lead? It all starts with allowing the Holy Spirit to take over your heart, and determining to keep it submitted to Him:

*"For as he thinketh in his heart, so is he."* (Prov. 23:7a)

## Chapter 6
## ACCENTUATING THE POSITIVE

Maintaining a positive attitude is another of the Godly characteristics so needed by extraordinary leaders.

The Word gives us specific instructions as to how to think:

*"Finally, brethren, whatsoever things are true, whatsoever things are honest, whatsoever things are just, whatsoever things are pure, whatsoever things are lovely, whatsoever things are of good report; if there be any virtue, and if there be any praise, think on these things. Those things, which ye have both learned, and received, and heard, and seen in me, do: and the God of peace shall be with you."* (Phil. 4:8-9)

It is obvious, by the fact that the Apostle Paul felt we needed to be told this, that the Lord knows there will be plenty of things to think of that do not fit in the above categories.

We live, just as the apostles of old did, in a world full of negativity, skepticism, bitterness, criticism, unforgiveness, backbiting, and gossip. That is why he says IF there is any virtue, IF there is any praise, think on these things. He knows we may sometimes have to look pretty hard to find the lovely, the pure, the just and the virtuous – even in the church!

His goal is to get us to focus on what is good, and if there is nothing else we can always think of Jesus and His love and sacrifice for us.

To be a leader who makes an impact on those lives around us, on society and on the Church, we must always look at the glass as half-full, not half empty. We must trust the vision God has given us so absolutely that no matter how negative the circumstances look, no matter how difficult the situation may be we can look forward to the victory at the fulfillment of that vision.

**Turn Negatives Into Positives**

It extends to our personal lives and conversations too, as well as our vision.

We must be very careful about coming into agreement with negativism, especially about our peers.

One day a friend came to visit me at home. As we talked about what a joy it was to be in Christ and shared testimonies of His goodness, she began to relate something she had heard about someone else, a sister in the body of Christ.

Her comments were negative ones, and my first reaction was to ask her how she knew these things were true. When she began to tell me that she didn't really know for sure, that these were just things she had heard, I stopped her cold.

I warned her that she had evidently already taken sides, in spite of having no proof of the accusations, and was, by mentioning it, passing the negativity on to me. I told her if she had doubts she needed to go to that person to find out what she would say in her defense.

I suggested that since the subject had, unfortunately, been brought up, we should pray for that person. We prayed that if there was any truth to the rumor that God would deal with her and correct her, and if there was no truth that God would vindicate her.

Either way the goal was not to find the fault and spread negative rumors, but to help the person to be able to keep moving ahead in the call that God has placed on her life.

I always like to remember the example of King David who, even knowing that King Saul wanted to murder him, would not put his mouth or his sword on him, and even rebuked those around him for wanting to (see 1 Sam. 24). He took seriously, as should we, the warning to "touch not God's anointed." (see 1 Chron. 16:22)

## Accentuating the Positive

A good leader does not walk in negativity towards team members, but will cover them, encourage them and correct them. An impact leader must be willing to display the same loyalty to their team members as they expect to have displayed towards them.

Instead of criticizing, humility looks for a way to bring out the best in someone else, knowing that Christ has extended the same to us.

**When Rebuke Is Necessary**

While always determining to keep a Godly attitude, and thinking the best of those who are working with us to fulfill the vision, it is sometimes apparent that there are problems.

Sometimes there will be a person who started out with a pure heart and motive who, because they gave in to their flesh, have turned away from a Godly lifestyle and are no longer walking the kind of walk necessary to accomplish things for the Kingdom alongside of you or under your authority.

It could be that they have simply refused to mature, keeping selfish motives instead of "team" objectives. It might be that they simply can't keep their word. It may be that they have fallen into sexual sin, or become entangled in old addictions or emotional bondages. Or it might be that their pride has reared its ugly head and they think they should still walk with you in ministry, but not submit to your leadership.

**Correction Will Tell**

Here is where we need to look at Biblical wisdom to know how to deal with situations. The Word says in Proverbs 9:8-9 that if you rebuke a wise man he will love you for it, but if you reprove a scorner he will hate you.

How a person reacts to your correction will tell you whether he is walking as a person of Godly wisdom or not.

# Becoming an Extraordinary Leader

There should be a very deep, covenant fellowship established between a true impact leader and those who are called to walk with them to fulfill the vision. If one of those who has been working with you in the fulfillment of the vision falls away from the Lord, or begins to walk in rebellion to the Word or to your leadership you must heed the Apostle Paul's advice:

*"And have no fellowship with the unfruitful works of darkness, but rather reprove them."* (Eph. 5:11)

It may be as simple as learning that they are questioning your ability or leadership and discussing it with others behind your back. It may be as complex as finding out that they are cheating on their spouse, or abusing their children.

Obviously the ideal answer, if a team member is showing signs of sin or rebellion, is that you take that person aside, confront the issue, give them wisdom from the Word and lead them to repentance. Then you can pray together for God's wisdom on what acts of forgiveness or restitution need to be done and move ahead from there, in stronger covenant than ever.

## Taking Painful Positive Steps

On the other hand, if they refuse to meet with you to discuss an issue, refuse to listen to your counsel, or will not act on Godly correction, you must consider that they are not willing to be obedient to your leadership and therefore do not belong on your team.

It can be personally painful to have to release a team member, particularly if in the past they seemed a very valuable covenant partner in your vision. But, it goes beyond personal feelings. It goes deep down to the covenant commitment you have with the Lord to fulfill the vision He has given you.

You cannot afford to taint the vision God has given you to fulfill by trying to continue in fellowship with those who are determined to link up with the "unfruitful works of darkness," which certainly include rebellion.

## Releasing – A Positive Stand

As negative as this may sound, it is actually a positive step. In releasing those who may hinder your ministry or the unity of the team who work with you, you are taking a very positive stand to show that the purity of the vision must be maintained, regardless of the cost. You will also be showing appreciation to those who have been loyal and submissive to your leadership.

You will even be doing something positive for the person who has been released, because you are giving them the opportunity to seek God as to the truth in what you tried to teach them during your confrontation.

If they were indeed called to be a part of your ministry the Lord may bring them to a place of repentance and forgiveness and bring them back to you. If they were misplaced to begin with, the Lord can, if they are willing, deal with them and place them in the position He intends them to be to fulfill their calling.

Using your God-given wisdom and authority as an impact leader, you must take every positive step, even the difficult ones, to keep the vision pure and untainted.

## Don't Look at Their Faces

As a called leader you will have enemies who will do all they can to seed negativity into your heart and mind. Even weak believers can be used of the enemy when they are operating in the flesh and say things that are intended to stir up doubt and unbelief.

I am personally in covenant with several trusted leaders that I can consult concerning my own vision, and I am grateful for their sound, Biblical counsel. But, ultimately, it is not what any person says regarding your vision, even those you love and trust the most. Your God-given vision is His vision, and He is the one who will use you to bring it to pass if you don't allow doubt or fear to get in your way.

Keep a positive attitude. God is with you, He has given you a mighty vision, and He is big enough to bring it to pass in spite of your shortcomings or the negative things that will be hurled at you and the ministry.

It would do you well, as you step out to fulfill your God-given call as a leader to impact people, a church, a community or the nations, to remember, even write it down and post it where you can see it daily, the assurance the Lord gave His servant Jeremiah:

*"Be not afraid of their faces: for I am with thee to deliver thee, saith the LORD."* (Jer. 1:8)

Being assured of God's faithfulness is the surest way to maintain a positive attitude, and be able to keep in the Spirit and accent the positive, in spite of circumstances and surroundings.

## Chapter 7
## LEADING FROM YOUR KNEES

As you grow into a true leader, and begin to raise up others with the potential for impact leadership, you must begin to appreciate the importance of prayer in your life and ministry as never before.

One snare into which the enemy will try to pull a busy leader is the trap of believing that once you are in a position of leadership you can leave the praying to the ministry intercessors and concentrate on "more important" things. Nothing could be farther from the truth.

Of course you want to encourage those around you to be watchful in prayer, and open to what the Lord speaks to them, but that is no substitute for your own one-on-one leadership conferences with the Boss of the operation.

A true impact leader must lead from their knees.

The same essential prayer life that raised you up in the Lord, the same reliance on the leading of the Holy Spirit through times of meditation on the Word, will become even more essential to a leader of impact as their influence increases.

**Keeping Prayer a Priority**

As your schedule becomes more and more crowded, your responsibilities become greater and greater, and your influence becomes more widespread, your flesh may rise up and try to talk you into the fact that you "don't have time" for the same kind of prayer life you enjoyed before. You must determine to keep your communication with God a priority.

One essential thing you must remember is that no matter how big and important you become in the eyes of those you lead, you are still no more capable of accomplishing anything of value by yourself, through your flesh, than you ever were. Remember Jesus' words in John 15:5: "...Without me you can do nothing." They are just as true for leadership as they are for the newest believer.

**IT IS TRUE YOU ARE NO LONGER DEPENDENT ON GOD THE SAME WAY YOU WERE BEFORE – YOU NEED TO BE FAR MORE DEPENDENT THAN EVER!**

Not only should you "lead from your knees" by constantly being in communication with the Lord over each step of ministry development, but you must remain prayerful in order to keep yourself personally on the right track – always growing more and more Christ-like, rather than more like a corporate business leader.

**Pray for Those You Lead**

Another aspect of your prayer life that must increase rather than decrease is the time you spend in prayer for those over which you have been given delegated authority. Consider Jesus, and His prayer for His disciples in John 17. Even the Son of God realized that if the leaders He had raised up were to have impact He must do more than be an example alongside them – He must also keep them lifted up before the Father.

The Apostle Paul put this into practice, as well:

*"Wherefore also we pray always for you, that our God would count you worthy of this calling, and fulfill all the good pleasure of his goodness, and the work of faith with power: That the name of our Lord Jesus Christ may be glorified in you, and ye in him, according to the grace of our God and the Lord Jesus Christ."* (2 Thess. 1:11,12)

## Importance of Corporate Prayer

Corporate prayer is a vital foundation for any church or ministry. When the leaders and congregation gather regularly to approach the throne boldly together, you can be assured that you are staying on the best path toward fulfilling the vision God has given you.

Many pastors and ministry leaders complain that they can't get the people to gather for prayer. They may have 1000 people in the congregation and only 15 show up for corporate prayer meetings. There are two comments I'd like to make about that.

One, the corporate prayer meeting is the place to "scout" for potential leaders. Those who attend most regularly are your "leadership job pool," so to speak. Who better to delegate responsibility to than to those whose prayer life shows they recognize they don't know it all, but know Who has the answers.

## Taking an Active Role

A true leader will not be "too busy" to attend at least some of the prayer meetings themselves, even though they may have delegated leadership over those meetings to a trusted subordinate.

Not only is occasional personal attendance a powerful way to lead by example, but it allows those who are called to work around you to get a more intimate look at who you are as a child of God.

Two, because human nature tends to put people on pedestals, it is important that those who walk with you in ministry, while they see the power and anointing of God on your life, not see you as larger than life.

Try just showing up at a prayer meeting, not to take over, but just to pray in agreement with those you lead.

Being publicly vulnerable in prayer is a great way for the people who have been gathered around you by the Lord to see that you are not some egomanic demi-god, but a humble servant, called to leadership, who is truly asking them to "Follow me as I follow Jesus," like the Apostle Paul did.

**Hearing God's Voice**

An impact leader must be willing and able to hear the voice of God:

*"My sheep hear my voice, and I know them, and they follow me."* (John 20:27)

*"And a stranger will they not follow, but will flee from him, for they know not the voice of strangers."* (John 10:5)

So, as you can see, God has promised to speak to His people. The promise goes on to say that we will hear His voice. But we must spend time with Him, in order to be listening to what He is saying for us, day by day.

It is by listening to His voice that we can receive our instructions, step by step, to be sure we are in the center of His will, both for our own lives and for the ministry and people over which He has given us leadership:

*"And thine ears shall hear a word behind thee, saying, This is the way, walk ye in it, when ye turn to the right hand, and when ye turn to the left."* (Isa. 30:21 )

Becoming a truly extraordinary leader will mean continually seeking out God, and recognizing that spending time with Him, in prayer and in His Word, is a vital necessity. You will truly be "leading from your knees."

## Chapter 8
## ANSWERING THE APOSTOLIC CALL

God is placing an apostolic call on His leadership. This calling is an instruction or authorization given to the Church for the spreading of the Gospel by becoming a training, equipping, and sending mechanism for the end times.

As part of this apostolic calling, God is sending out a sound of recall to the church to return to the laying on of hands reproduction system we witnessed in the book of Acts, and throughout the New Testament Scriptures.

*"Now there were in the church that was at Antioch certain prophets and teachers; as Barnabas, and Simeon that was called Niger, and Lucius of Cyrene, and Manaen, which had been brought up with Herod the tetrarch, and Saul. As they ministered to the Lord, and fasted, the Holy Ghost said, Separate me Barnabas and Saul for the work whereunto I have called them. And when they had fasted and prayed, and laid their hands on them, they sent them away."* (Acts 13:1-3)

*"Wherefore I put thee in remembrance that thou stir up the gift of God, which is in thee by the putting on of my hands."* (2 Tim. 1:6)

### Led by the Holy Spirit

We should note that the "laying on of hands" to send someone out into ministry was not done lightly. The "separation" of Barnabas and Saul was initiated by the Holy Spirit, not by the church leaders.

It was not a decision made by a committee of elders, nor simply a reward for the completion of any certain classes or training. The leadership had done their part to train and raise them up, and Barnabas and Saul had proved themselves faithful, but they still only sent them forth by the laying on of hands when the Holy Spirit gave them the unction. Even then, it was not done without fasting and prayer.

While it is crucial for us as leaders to adopt this God-given method of laying on of hands to launch into ministry or to activate the gifts in potential leaders, it is important that we do so using God's guidelines. We must not do it recklessly, haphazardly, or by man's formulas. We are admonished to lay hands suddenly on no man (see 1 Tim. 5:22). There is a vital impartation involved in the laying on of hands, rather like the "passing of the mantle" from Elijah to Elisha. It is to be done only when we have been assured by the Holy Spirit that the person is indeed not only chosen, but properly prepared spiritually and naturally to step into a position of active ministry leadership.

**The Apostolic Calling vs. Called Apostles**

Many of you have read my book "Who Me, Prophesy?" where I discuss the difference between operating in the gift of prophecy and being called to the office of a prophet. There is a parallel here, when it comes to an apostolic calling, which needs to be clearly understood. While all anointed leaders can operate in an apostolic calling, and impart gifts and launch others into ministry as the Holy Spirit leads them, not all leaders are called to the office of an apostle.

One major difference can be seen very clearly in the Biblical accounts of the early church. Planted appointed and anointed leaders of a local assembly can be moved to lay hands and launch members of their flock into ministry (as it was in Antioch in the verses above from Acts 13). Those who were the called apostles did not permanently plant themselves in a church, although they had a base of operations, but went to areas where ministry was needed.

Once there they worked with the called evangelist and spread the Gospel, forming a nucleus of believers into a church. They worked with those believers until it was apparent who in that local body was called to leadership. They trained those potential leaders and raised them up and, when the Holy Spirit showed them that they were ready, they laid hands on them and commissioned them to take over leadership of that body. Then the called apostle moved on to the next area to which the Holy Spirit called him, and the process began again.

While the apostles remained actively interested in the health and growth of the new church, they passed on the pastoral leadership roles, and merely acted as spiritual advisors and counselors to the church. Most of the Apostle Paul's letters were his "advisory counseling," so to speak, to the leaders he had placed in the various churches he had planted.

The apostolic leader is planted in a church or ministry. The called apostle plants churches and ministries.

**The Cry for Apostolic Leadership**

During my travels in ministry, I am hearing the sound of church members wanting more training for moving in the gifts of the Holy Spirit in order to reach out to those that are lost, sick, and dying. God is placing a hunger in His people to desire more of His anointing to be imparted through leadership.

While being driven to the airport after a recent three-day ministry engagement, the driver confided in me, as well as a well-known author and friend, that she had learned more and been offered more of an opportunity to use her gifts in those three days than she had in all the years she had been in her home church.

In another instance, at the end of my first session out of five on "Ministering in the Gifts," a woman ran up to me, bursting with excitement, saying, "This has been so good! I felt a confidence rise up in me and fear lift off of me." She continued, "It is rare to find a minister willing to teach, train and activate the gifts God has placed in you. They usually only talk about it."

It is a sad commentary on the neglect of the leadership to answer the apostolic call.

For the past century church leaders, for the most part, have dropped the ball when it comes to operating in an apostolic call. It is time for us, today's chosen leaders, to pick up and begin to take responsibility for stirring up the gifts in those we lead, and encouraging them to operate in the believers anointing, as we will be discussing. It means we must not only take the time to train and edify, but we must be in good communication with the Holy Spirit to know when His timing is right to lay hands and activate their giftings.

This does not, of course, take the responsibility away from the believer for spending quality time in God's Word themselves, nor excuse them from spending precious time with Him to hear God's marching orders for their own lives. However, leadership is also receiving the call to come up higher in the realm of impartation and activation.

As leaders, we must begin to move in response to this God-given apostolic call.

## Section II

## IMPACTING OTHERS TO LEAD

## Chapter 9
## MODELING RESPECT FOR AUTHORITY

As a called leader in the body of Christ, you have been given a great responsibility. But in order to carry out the responsibility God has called you to, He has also given you the necessary authority. It is important that you show those you lead the importance of authority by being a model of respect for those in authority over you.

Operating "decently and in order" and in delegated authority is a foundational basis for extraordinary impact leadership.

God is the ultimate authority, and has absolute control.

Do not confuse control with authority. God delegates His authority to His chosen people, but He does not relinquish or delegate His control to anyone.

One reason there is strife and division in the body of Christ today is that too many leaders are trying to control those placed under them, instead of acting in God's delegated authority to lead them. It amazes me how some leaders can think that just because they are Godly men, called to leadership, that they have the right to exercise control.

### Jesus Walked in Delegated Authority

Even Jesus Himself had to relinquish His right to control to come in the flesh, and He operated in delegated authority while on earth:

*"Then said Jesus unto them, When ye have lifted up the Son of man, then shall ye know that I am he, and that I do nothing of myself; but as my Father hath taught me, I speak these things. And he that sent me is with me: the Father hath not left me alone; for I do always those things that please him."* (John 8:28-29)

If this isn't a pattern for even those of us in highest positions of leadership to follow, I don't know what is! When we say that we want to be like Jesus it means we are willing to walk in delegated authority, not allowing our carnal mind to take control, but always doing only what the Father has taught – things that will please Him.

## Exercising Authority

Yet, even though Jesus was only operating in delegated authority, there was still no doubt that He did have the right to exercise that authority:

*"And they were astonished at his doctrine: for he taught them as one that had authority, and not as the scribes."* (Mark 1:22)

As we operate in impact leadership, with the delegated authority given to us by God, we will be able to, and indeed must, exercise whatever authority is needed to fulfill our God-given vision.

Moses had Godly leadership counsel from Jethro on how to use his delegated authority:

*"Hearken now unto my voice, I will give thee counsel, and God shall be with thee: Be thou for the people to God-ward, that thou mayest bring the causes unto God: And thou shalt teach them ordinances and laws, and shalt shew them the way wherein they must walk, and the work that they must do."* (Exo. 18:19-20)

## A Lesson in Leadership

Paul gave Timothy a great lesson in leadership:

*"Exhort servants to be obedient unto their own masters, and to please them well in all things, not answering again; Not purloining, but shewing all good fidelity; that they may adorn the doctrine of God our Saviour in all things. ...These things speak, and exhort, and rebuke with all authority. Let no man despise thee."* (Titus 2:9-10, 15)

## Modeling Respect for Authority

He made it clear that, as the leader, it was Timothy's job to teach those he lead to respect authority, including his own.

## Delegating Authority to Others

But notice something very important about the example of Jesus. He operated in delegated authority, but in that position He was still able to not only exercise authority, but to delegate authority to those he was leading:

> *"Then he called his twelve disciples together, and gave them power and authority over all devils, and to cure diseases. And he sent them to preach the kingdom of God, and to heal the sick."* (Luke 9:1-2)

## Respecting Authority

As I stated earlier, God has ultimate authority. Since we love and respect our Heavenly Father, respecting authority is a must for all believers.

Our first responsibility, of course, is to respect God's authority as we have learned it in His Word. But we also have a responsibility to respect those to whom God has delegated authority:

> *"Obey them that have the rule over you, and submit yourselves: for they watch for your souls, as they that must give account, that they may do it with joy, and not with grief: for that is unprofitable for you."* (Heb. 13:17)

Paul was so concerned about respecting the ruling authorities that when he found himself in conflict with Ananias he said that he wished Ananias were not a high priest, because he had to obey the law that said, "Thou shalt not speak evil of the ruler." (read Acts 23:5)

David was another Biblical example of this when he refused to kill Saul, even though he had become a mortal enemy, because he knew God's law warned him to "touch not God's anointed."

As an impact leader you become one of those that it references in Hebrews who "must give account" for the obedience of those you lead. But Paul's and David's examples of respecting even evil authority is an important example of God's mandate that no matter how great a leader you are, you must respect others in positions of authority above your own, even while teaching others to respect your authority.

**The Military Model**

Often, when talking of the order of God, a military parallel can clarify our understanding.

Those that are in, or have been in, the military recognize the principle of file and ranking. They understand that the system is set up in such a way that the only possibility of advancement comes from learning how to respect authority and follow the commands or instruction of their delegated leaders.

There is, of course, a Commander-in-Chief, but although he has ultimate responsibility for the outcome of the battles, he delegates his authority to his generals.

They obey his orders and then delegate their authority to lesser officers. They again obey their orders and then delegate their authority to platoon leaders, etc., until finally the orders are carried out.

In the course of preparing for and fighting the battles, each level of soldier must be drilled in how to march together, taught how to use the weapons available, taught to respect the authority over them, and instructed, emotionally and physically, in how to win.

They recognize the importance of obeying orders from their direct leader, because they know that leader is following and passing along the orders of those farther up the line, and that ultimately there is a Commander-in-Chief with an overall battle plan.

The individual footsoldier may not be aware of the strategy of their positioning, but they trust the delegated authority

## Modeling Respect for Authority

over them who tells them which way to march. Their leaders, in turn, may see only a slightly larger portion of the overall strategy, but also have trust and confidence in the delegated authority from whom they are receiving orders.

### Teaching Our Troops

Many times ministers don't realize that as a teaching mechanism we need to teach our troops just like the military to be able to stand in rank, how to march, how to win, and how to handle the weapons that are given to them. They need to know how to fire those machine guns and rifles, how to not break rank in combat, or it is detrimental to all. Some could even lose their lives.

The leaders that makes an impact on the troops in the military are not necessarily those high-ranking ones who get the ultimate blame or credit. The greatest impact is made by those trainers, those squadron leaders, those who run alongside the troops to help them get into physical condition, those who organize the new recruits and make them able to execute in order to be victorious.

### The Need for Respect & Obedience

In Christian ministry it would do well for us to use the military model when it comes to understanding the need for learning to respect and obey delegated authority. Unfortunately, our society has bred such a democratic system that it has caused a false freedom breakdown,

Just as in the military it is the recruit who learns to follow instructions faithfully, with confidence in the delegated authority over them, who in turn is promoted and becomes a leader, so it will be in God's delegated authority in the body of Christ.

There are many highly anointed individuals, with a call to great leadership, who have fallen short of fulfilling their destiny, perhaps even fallen away from the Lord, because they took their leadership call and perverted it to think they were now so high ranking they didn't need to listen to anyone else. At best they stand to lose their destiny. At worst, these "loose cannons" can be dangerous to themselves and others.

Take your leadership position seriously, but remember your authority is delegated authority, not absolute. Always stay mindful of the instructions of the Holy Spirit, and always march forward in rank, willing to listen to those whom God has placed in leadership over you, and teaching respect for authority to those over whom He has given you delegated authority.

## Chapter 10
## LEADING BY EXAMPLE

The Apostle Paul refers in Corinthians to believers as "epistles," read by all men. It is even more prevalent for leaders, because others tend to look to us as examples. Our words, our writings, our teachings may be valuable, but it is the example we set with our actions and attitudes that will make us truly extraordinary leaders.

When we set a good example we impact others who in turn will "reproduce" and impact others, who will then become examples. Paul tells how this worked in his ministry:

*"And ye became followers of us, and of the Lord, having received the word in much affliction, with joy of the Holy Ghost: So that ye were ensamples to all that believe in Macedonia and Achaia. For from you sounded out the word of the Lord not only in Macedonia and Achaia, but also in every place your faith to God-ward is spread abroad; so that we need not to speak any thing."* (1 Thess. 1:6)

**People are Watching**

One thing a Christian leader must always remain aware of is that people are watching. They are watching virtually every move you make, and you cannot afford to let your guard down when it comes to exemplifying Godly behavior and character traits.

The examples we set as leaders will live beyond the moment, whether good or bad. In Paul's case his example caused many others to spread the Gospel. I heard one comment that shows how a negative example lives on, as well.

After excitedly telling me all she had learned by the "hands-on" teaching I had been giving, a woman commented, "It is rare to find a minister willing to teach, train and activate the gifts God has placed in you. They usually only talk about it."

What a sad commentary on hypocritical leadership who expect people to "do as they say, and not as they do."

**Follow Me as I Follow Jesus**

As impact leaders today we should instead be like the Apostle Paul, who had no problem telling his followers to look to him as an example:

*"Brethren, be followers together of me, and mark them which walk so as ye have us for an ensample."* (Phil. 3:17)

The Apostle Peter exhorted his leaders to beware of "lording over" the people, but instead to humble themselves to become an example:

*"The elders which are among you I exhort, who am also an elder, and a witness of the sufferings of Christ, and also a partaker of the glory that shall be revealed: Feed the flock of God which is among you, taking the oversight thereof, not by constraint, but willingly; not for filthy lucre, but of a ready mind; Neither as being lords over God's heritage, but being ensamples to the flock."* (1 Peter 5:1-3)

Just about every great leader had someone who poured into their life. Elijah poured into Elisha. Paul poured into Timothy. Football, baseball, basketball coaches pour into those up and coming into fame.

The world refers to this personal impact leadership as mentoring. Mentors are those who take another under their wing and teach them from their experience and example. The difference, of course, in Christian mentors or leaders is that they will teach them from the Word, and the examples found

# Leading by Example

there, as well as from their personal experiences and example.

## Mentoring Makes a Difference

Often the counsel and encouragement of a good leader or mentor will make the difference between someone being a success or a failure.

For a new believer, the presence of a good mentor may make the difference between whether or not that person will be able to walk and live victoriously in the Lord and fulfill their destiny.

The person doing the mentoring may not always be the one who makes it to the top, or gains the public success, but those at the top often publicly acknowledge those who ran with them, poured into them and pressed them from behind.

Extraordinary leaders should not only be committed themselves, but should demonstrate that commitment so well that others desire to follow. Elijah demonstrated Godly power with such authority that Elisha was compelled to keep by his side until the end of Elijah's ministry.

Elisha saw how God worked miraculously through Elijah to see His purposes fulfilled and knowing he had been trained well, he had no problem knowing that God could and would use him just as powerfully.

Even the military recognizes the importance of a good example. A drill sergeant in boot camp not only gives the orders during the physical exercises, he demonstrates as he runs alongside the troops...keeping them motivated in their efforts.

Even though the Lord has set up a "ranking" system of sorts, to help bring about His perfect order, today's leaders must be willing to step out of the comfort zone of being "the minister" and allow themselves to be an example to the others God is wanting to use them to train for leadership.

The examples we set as leaders will determine how effective those we train will become. Once again we see how vastly different things must be in the Lord than in the world. A worldly leader, as long as he fulfills his prescribed duties, can be as morally corrupt, as lacking in integrity, as dishonest in business, or as abusive at home as he feels like being. It is just not so in the Kingdom of God.

As a leader representing the Lord Jesus Christ, desiring to make an impact on those God puts under our sphere of influence, our attitudes and lifestyle are as important a part of our leadership as our messages, our words of prophecy, or our ability to draw a crowd or take an offering. We must first and foremost be an example of the character of Jesus. That is what will make us extraordinary. That is what will have an impact.

## Chapter 11
## FLOWING IN THE BELIEVER'S ANOINTING

In the end-times we can see where the Lord is beginning to bring the five-fold ministry into an even greater level of cooperation with one another. All across America there is growing talk about denominations coming together and different churches beginning to work in unity to see God's work being done.

But God truly has a plan and a purpose for His people. Even though man's plan might seem to be a good one, the Lord has His plan. The five-fold ministry are the equipping ones, they are the gifts that were sent to the body by Jesus Christ when He ascended into heaven (see Eph. 4). When they are brought into unity and cooperation, God's purposes and plans will come to pass.

Church history reveals many varied movements of God throughout the centuries. In the early 1900's it was the faith, charismatic, Pentecostal movements. In the 1980's it was the prophetic movement, and in the 1990's the apostolic movement. When you look historically at how God has orchestrated these movements it becomes apparent that they have each been steps toward bringing the apostles, prophets, pastors, evangelists, and teachers back into His Divine order, so that the work He has planned shall come to pass.

This next great movement of God is the saint's movement. We are now actually in a third church millennium, and God has plans for us to retain all the previous movements and now ignite the everyday believer in Christ to go out and do His work, so Jesus will come a second time and we will all go home. But, He is coming for a glorious church without spot or wrinkle. In order for that to take place the "believers' anointing" must be activated, and the saints have to begin to move into the things God has called and predestined them to move in.

## The Anointing Is for All Believers

Every practicing believer (one who actively seeks out God through His Word and is developing a relationship with Him) has a certain portion of anointing flowing through them, activated by the Holy Spirit.

*"For there is no difference between the Jew and the Greek: for the same Lord over all is rich unto all that call upon him."* (Romans 10:12)

*"But the anointing which ye have received of him abideth in you, and ye need not that any man teach you: but as the same anointing teacheth you of all things, and is truth, and is no lie, and even as it hath taught you, ye shall abide in him."* (1 John 2:27)

The word "anointing" in the Greek is chrisma; a smearing, an endowment, an unction, an anointing of the Holy Spirit. The anointing is the manifested presence of the Holy Spirit.

The only way we can truly lead others to Him or lead others into leadership is to lead by the unction of Jesus Christ which comes through the Holy Spirit, Who is always ready to help us be about the Father's business.

This is where we must be willing to offer God our natural abilities and faith so that He can combine them with His supernatural abilities, so that we can help others reach their potential.

## Fulfilling the Great Commission

Jesus spoke more than once to His disciples of what was to happen to them and what was expected of them when He went to the Father. The best known is probably what we refer to as "The Great Commission" found in Matthew 28:19-20, and Mark 16:15-20.

He said, *"Teaching them to observe everything that I have commanded you, and behold, I am with you all the days."*

## Flowing in the Believers' Anointing

This is His commission to us, as leaders today, just as it was His commission to those He was then placing into leadership. We must not only do what He has taught us, but we are responsible to teach others to do those things as well!

Jesus goes on to tell us to:

*"And he said unto them, Go ye into all the world, and preach the gospel to every creature."* (Mark 16:15)

As leaders we should expect to become examples of *Joel 2:28-29*:

*"And afterward I will pour out My Spirit upon all flesh; and your sons and daughters shall prophesy, your old men shall dream dreams, your young men shall see visions. Even upon the menservants and upon the maidservants in those days will I pour out My Spirit."*

We must recognize that we may have been appointed to leadership, but God expects us to lead those who are often left setting in the pews into an understanding of the power they have been given by the Holy Spirit in them, and the responsibilities they have as believers to also walk and work in His anointing.

As impact leaders we must be intentional in our efforts to give those we lead, especially the potential leaders, the opportunity to not only learn but also to put into practice what they are being taught. It is our responsibility to not only operate in our own "believers' anointing," but to do all we can to encourage, nurture and stir it up in those we lead, and even, at times, build a platform for them to grow in confidence and gain in experience.

The Holy Spirit anoints leaders to pour into others and raise them up. God is always willing to impart and send. The question is, are we ready to make the sacrifices it entails?

**Are We Ready?**

Are we ready to help people at their time of need, even when the phone rings when we're not in the mood to minister to someone? Are we willing to walk in humility and sacrifice to do what God has called us to do? We must be if we are to be extraordinary leaders who will impact others to lead.

Our God is in the people business, therefore we must be in the people business.

We cannot carry an anointing and be haughty. We cannot carry an anointing and say, "Look at me." We're to lead in humility, and with love. 1 Cor. 13 says it is like a clanging cymbal if we don't minister with love. We can't minister to others with a harsh or dictatorial authority or with a critical spirit, for God said the first commandment was to love Him and the next was to love your neighbor as yourself.

As leaders we must be especially diligent and prepared to live the Word, so we can stir others to live the Word.

At times the anointing within a believer lies dormant. One natural parallel would be to consider what it's like when you've eaten a big meal. If you give in to the natural temptation to curl up with the Word, or sprawl in the easy chair and watch television, you will fall asleep. If, instead, you wait a bit, then get up and begin moving (take a walk, for example), the action will help the meal digest and it will cause you to have the energy needed to accomplish something more with your day or evening.

**Waking a Sleeping Church**

Likewise, when you have been "fed" a good meal from the bread of the Word, instead of just taking it in and going nowhere with it, if you get moving and begin to put the revelation you received to work, you will begin to feel stirred in the anointing and activated by the revelation.

The Word commands us to "Wake thou that sleepest" (see Eph. 5:14), and begin to walk wisely, not as fools.

As leaders we can see when the body of Christ is in transition, stagnant, or dormant. Our call is to pray - asking God to show us our part in helping bring transition or break the demonic assignment that may be holding the body captive. Remember that the Word tells us that the harvest is ripe, but it's the laborers that are few.

When we pray for those harvest workers, as leaders, we must then be ready to be used to help raise them up and encourage them to be all they have been anointed to be for the Lord, whether at home, in their neighborhood, on the job, or in public ministry positions.

Unfortunately, too many of today's leaders are not using the anointing they have in leadership to stir and nurture the "believers' anointing" in those sitting under their leadership.

Too many Christians sit in congregations listening to anointed leaders, taking copious notes. They've been exposed to Gospel principles and leave with "head knowledge," but too often that is the end of their experience. As impact leaders we must help them discover ways to take what they are learning and put it to use to further God's Kingdom.

**Stepping up to the Plate**

While being driven to the airport after a recent three-day ministry engagement, the driver confided in me that she had learned more and been offered more of an opportunity to use her gifts in those three days than she had in her home church in the previous three or four months.

This ought never to be the confession of an active believer. Today's leaders must "step up to the plate," as it were, and begin to activate that believers' anointing that has been ignored or neglected.

**From "Knowing" to "Doing" to "Growing"**

One way to help those you are leading put the wisdom or revelation you are sharing into practice is to give them an assignment related to the message. This advances the "knowing" into "doing" and then into "growing."

For instance, to help them think and respond in a practical way, one leader taught on mentoring, then challenged his audience to write to someone who had played an important role in his or her life as a mentor. Expressing thanks to one who had contributed to his or her Christian growth not only stirred gratitude, but putting it on paper helped them recognize what it took to be a mentor.

Challenging and stirring the believer's anointing also has a ripple effect. One friend of mine who received such a letter told me she cherishes it. It had been ten years since her family had taken a young man into their home for a year. He wrote to thank her for his opportunity to experience normal Christian family life. He said he had never before experienced family devotions and holiday celebrations, and it impacted his life.

Today the young man is a pastor with three children of his own and he's integrated what he learned from her family into his own home. The letter, coming so long after he'd moved out, meant a great deal to my friend. Had the speaker not given the assignment to thank a mentor would the young man have written that letter? Who knows. But the result was that the mentor could see the impact their life had made, and was still making ten years later.

There is another step we, as leaders, must take beyond helping potential leaders become stirred in their anointing. In order to make an impact beyond our church and into our community, or even on a national and global level, we must begin to disciple and nurture those who are in the workplace.

**Taking It to the Workplace**

For too many years those in the marketplace (whether as a clerk in a retail store or the CEO of an international corporation) have felt they had no place in ministry. But the fact is that there are many called and anointed believers who hold full-time positions in the world of business. Some have an anointing to be a shepherd in that arena, others an anointing to be a prophet or apostle in that arena. There is no reason these believers cannot seek God and gain His wisdom for ministering in the marketplace.

Some may begin to see even the nature of their job evolving into a ministry and step into their God-given destiny without ever leaving their business or office.

**No One Left Out**

God has an individual destiny for each of us in His kingdom and His desire is that no one is left out. So it becomes our responsibility, as leaders impacting others, to nurture and encourage these believers in the workplace, as faithfully as we would those with a desire for pulpit ministry as their vocation.

One day a believer came to me, concerned that she wasn't able to be active in church. She asked, "What can I do? I have a call to hospital work and I'm on a rotating shift and rarely have time to serve in church in any capacity, even though my heart is there. I tithe there, and I like to be there but I rarely have time to be in service there."

She had been hearing the message on the "believers' anointing" and was trying to make it make sense for her. "Does this mean that God has something special for me? How can I do it all?"

My reply to her was to assure her that the Lord had already placed her in her place of calling, and was allowing her to walk in her believers' anointing. "When you speak about your job you glow all over," I told her. "The Holy Spirit illuminates you and you begin to share wisdom and relate what happened to a person you prayed for, or how families have thanked you for being there to nurture and take care of their spouse or child. That is a work of ministry in itself."

She needed reassurance that not all ministry and service to the church has to take place within the four walls. "Know that as you use whatever God has given you, as you use the prayer or prophetic anointing within you, stay steadfast and diligently serve at that hospital as unto the Lord, you are serving Christ."

I also reminded her that God chose those who were in the workforce to accompany Him, and they became what we refer to today as His disciples. They began with their job skills and Jesus trained and discipled them until they became His Apostles–some to the church and some to the marketplace. When I had assured her that she was called, anointed, and appointed for Christ's work, and had been positioned in the workplace, her eyes lit up and she got so excited.

**"Just Doing My Job"**

She admitted, "I had never thought of it that way. I never knew that I could be considered a minister where I am every day, just doing my job, taking care of people." You could tell it gave her a whole new outlook on her walk with Christ.

As impact leaders we impact our world in even greater dimensions when we lead, teach, encourage, and nurture those who are called to ministry in their workplace to flow in their believers' anointing and recognize the importance of their placement to God.

Our responsibility is to raise up spiritual maturity, whether in those called to fulfill a five-fold ministry calling, those called to minister in the marketplace, or those called to minister love in their homes.

The believers' anointing – the incomparable anointing of the Holy Spirit of the Living God that we have been blessed to carry within us – is readily available, with all the power and authority it represents.

Let's grasp it, nurture it and put it to full use for ourselves as believers. And as leaders let's display it, share it, encourage and help develop its use in the lives of those over whom He has given us authority.

## Chapter 12
## REPRODUCING & RELEASING LEADERS

Now that we understand the anointing that the Holy Spirit places on believers, we need to discuss our responsibility as impact leaders moving into the apostolic anointing God has for His church.

We need to be willing to impart and activate the anointing in which we operate into others, in order to reproduce and multiply the true leadership we represent.

It is this reproduction phenomenon that will launch us on the path of preparation for the harvest.

**Jesus, Our Role Model**

Jesus is our role model. He reproduced Himself, and after they got baptized in the Holy Spirit, which Jesus asked them to wait for, His disciples became reproducers. It is a continuing cycle of reproduction.

Our goal is to become a leader after the heart of our Lord. Jesus Christ ministered to the multitudes, yet He spent valuable time with His disciples whom He trained to become apostles, who in turn trained up others.

*He said to His disciples, "The harvest is plentiful, but the workers are few. Therefore beseech the Lord of the harvest to send out workers into the harvest."*

*Then saith he unto his disciples, The harvest truly is plenteous, but the labourers are few; Pray ye therefore the Lord of the harvest, that he will send forth labourers into his harvest.* (Matt. 9:37-38)

The Apostle Paul understood the value of those in leadership reproducing, or multiplying themselves. He told those he discipled:

*"And the things that thou hast heard of me among many witnesses, the same commit thou to faithful men, who shall be able to teach others also."* (2 Tim. 2:2)

**The Impact of Leadership Reproduction**

The need for leadership to reproduce is necessary for the Gospel of the Lord Jesus Christ to continue to multiply.

In the days following the resurrection of Jesus, the demand for leadership was so great the disciples began to reproduce themselves not only in Jerusalem, but across the known world. You can read in Acts 6, and continue to see in Acts 7 and 8, how Phillip and Stephen showed a continuing increase of anointing upon their lives.

This type of reproduction caused such an increase in the Gospel of Jesus Christ that it caused those non-believing Jews who felt threatened by this influx to refer to the believers as "Those who have turned the world upside down." (see Acts 17:6)

Now that was having an impact!

As the leaders reproduce, their impact, as well as their number, will inevitably begin to multiply, and signs and wonders will be displayed which bring God glory.

**The Prime Ingredient**

A faithful member of our ministry team once asked, "What one ingredient would you say would help me to become a good leader?" My answer was, "To be an extraordinary leader, one who impacts others to lead, you must be willing to share what God has done to improve you and raise you up in leadership."

You must be willing to pass the teachings and anointing within you along to others. A good leader will motivate others by not only showing genuine concern and kindness,

## Reproducing and Releasing Leaders

but also making you feel that your participation is as crucial to accomplishing the work of ministry as their own.

I have personally been blessed with the opportunity to sit under extraordinary, quality leadership, who have modeled, encouraged, taught and imparted the doctrine of leadership reproduction in my life. I know it was a prime ingredient in my growth in ministry and leadership.

When I worked at the World Prayer Center in Colorado Springs, Colorado, my leadership were such clear examples of humility, honor, integrity, and character that I felt privileged to serve them. And they were willing to share with me in order that I could reproduce their kind of leadership in my life and ministry.

As we grow in leadership, we must be willing to talk, empower, act, and lead like a leader. There must also be the humility which stirs a sincere desire to reproduce.

This reproduction mentality will cause a multiplication that will perpetuate the releasing of anointings, developing literal armies of extraordinary leaders capable of handling the influx of the harvest as the Church progresses.

### Seeing Reproduction in Action

During the season my children and I had the privilege of serving at Church of the Harvest in Oklahoma City, under an anointed leader who impacted our lives by demonstrating reproduction in action. We learned how to continually work ourselves out of a position by raising others up to be positioned. Our pastor was intentional about launching this Biblical principle, and all benefited from it.

He made it a point to spend time with leadership as well as potential leadership, instilling into them the values of Biblical principles and the promises of God and allowing them to put them into practice. This reproduction system inevitably caused all involved to quickly rise to new levels.

# Becoming an Extraordinary Leader

The harvest began to pour in and the church grew from a congregation of under 100 people in 1991 to over 1,200 within five years. Because of the reproduction system in place, the saints had been positioned and were equipped to handle the influx of what God was doing.

I would venture to say that the success of Church of the Harvest is built on the premise that our pastor dared to recognize potential leaders, and spends time training them and developing relationships. This principle cannot afford to be ignored.

If we want to be impact leaders, we must learn to build people as sons and daughters in the Lord, nurturing them in their gifts through mentoring, and allowing their emerging gifts the room to flourish.

## Better Than a Hundred-Fold Return

It is amazing to watch what God can do when the principle of reproduction and multiplication are put into place. I have witnessed, through a friend of mine in Singapore, a better than hundred-fold return. Beginning with a group of 45, she has spent many years developing, training, equipping, and mentoring many of them to become leaders. This church has grown from a core group of less than 45 people to a congregation of about 5000 by applying the principle of seeing the potential God has placed within them, and nourishing it.

Now these leaders have begun to be launched to many other nations, and because of the dynamics of their training and witnessing they are continuing to develop, train, mentor, and release many others. This is a strong representation of the "great commission" in action.

## Multiplying Leadership

Multiplied numbers of people have been impacted because one extraordinary leader chose to develop potential, nurture gifts and callings, and release others to do what God has

## Reproducing and Releasing Leaders

called them to do. This is the great reproduction phenomenon of becoming an impact leader.

Another friend who works in international ministry training potential leaders recalls her training nearly 30 years ago. Her pastor felt God told him to pour himself into potential leaders in his church—to disciple them and teach them much of what he knew about the practicalities of leadership.

While some members were jealous because he did not personally disciple them, it wasn't possible with a congregation of more than 2,000 people, so he sought God on who he was to invest his time with. For six years this pastor invested in seven couples by teaching them in my friend's home every Sunday night after church.

### Simple Multiplication Reproduction

As a result every couple in that group agreed to open their homes to fourteen additional people each Wednesday night and teach them everything they had learned on Sunday night. Each one of them began to flow in portions of the believers' anointing.

This was simple multiplication reproduction in its best form.

Those in the Wednesday night groups were not all married couples, but included singles, widows, or even those married to unbelieving spouses. Many went on to become leaders in the church. Others found follow-up evangelism opportunities in their neighborhoods or workplaces.

For example, three of the men used their evangelism gifts one night a week in a nearby prison. Two took guitars to lead the singing, while one did the preaching. As these men went to the prison, their home group members were covering them in prayer.

The daily disciplines that this extraordinary pastor had required of those seven original couples in his Sunday night group, designed to make them healthy and complete in body, soul, and spirit, helped make them into true impact leaders.

Now, over thirty years later, my friend who was raised up during this process is still impacting leadership, training others in her international ministry.

There is a powerful "ripple effect" set in motion when a true leader devotes a portion of his or her ministry to seeding into potential leaders.

**Impartation by Laying on of Hands**

One aspect of the leadership reproduction process is to impart and release others into ministry by the laying on of hands.

In one Biblical example, Moses' father-in-law came to him and said (paraphrased), "Moses, you have too much to do. The people are pulling on you. It's time for you to release others into the ministry. It is time for you to designate to others to pick up portions of what you're doing."

When Moses heeded the advice and laid hands on the seventy it painted a strong picture for us in the Kingdom principle of the laying on of hands.

As he laid hands on them it served to help release that which is in them and put it to work. They began to pick up their portion of the mantle to build the Kingdom of God, allowing Moses to advance in what God had given him to do.

Another Biblical model is Paul with Timothy. Paul trained Timothy as he traveled with him in ministry. Then there came a day when Paul laid hands on Timothy so that his anointing could be released to enable Timothy to do what God had called him to do. We know that Timothy went on to do a great work for the Lord in his own right.

The impartation by laying on of hands is a wonderful way to begin to delegate others to help you carry the load of leadership.

## Reproducing and Releasing Leaders

When you publicly set forth certain members as potential leaders you are not only acknowledging them before the congregation, but you are also making a public declaration of your intention to give of yourself and your anointing to train and teach them to step forward into their positions of authority.

### Doing It God's Way

Since Jesus operated in leadership reproduction we know that it is God's way, and when we are obedient to do things God's way there is always a blessing or benefit involved. The parable of the ten talents, in Scripture, demonstrates the God-given principle that when you are faithful to use and increase the talents (gifts, anointings) God has given you, He will increase what you have.

I believe one reason some of the most powerfully used impact leaders on earth today are able to operate in such glorious levels of anointing and accomplish so much for the Kingdom of God is because they have been obedient to pass along the blessings through reproducing themselves.

Conversely, as demonstrated in the parable of the ten talents, when we bury the talents (gifts, anointings) we have been given, or hoard them for ourselves, we risk losing them altogether. That is a sobering thought!

Yet could this be what we are doing when we, out of love and respect for a newly groomed leader, resist letting them go and instead try to make them fit into our available space.

### Releasing Good Leaders

Most of us are familiar with the saying "You can't put a square peg in a round hole." Unfortunately, out of need for leadership in an area, we will sometimes assign a person with a specific gifting, such as ministry to children or to men, to another area because of a great need for leadership there.

It's true that we all, as part of our leadership growth and training, may be placed for a season in a position that is not the one we know God has ultimately called us to fill. However, no true leader should settle for being permanently affixed outside of their true God-given arena, neither should they expect a potential leader to permanently "adjust" to the area of greatest need and not continue toward their God-given call.

If a person's gifting is with women, for example, you need to lead them toward using that gifting to the fullest and teach them to focus on their calling to impact wives, mothers and women in the workplace. If your ministry doesn't really have such a position, are you willing to release that person to move on to a church or ministry who really has a need for their gifts?

Or, what happens when someone is very effectively ministering to women, but you recognize their anointing is becoming more generally apostolic or prophetic, suitable and needed for all in the body? You may use them in your women's ministry for a season, but don't make the mistake of tying them to "strictly women" simply because that's where your current leadership needs lie.

**Yet Another Exercise in Humility**

This is where a leader's gift of humility needs to come into play in a major way. We must truly put into practice the "in honor preferring one another" the Bible calls us to. It must become more important to us to see another leader find their ultimate God-given role than it is to keep our leadership team filled.

It is here our trust in the Lord is put to the test. Are we willing to release someone who is highly gifted and anointed, who has been a great asset and blessing to us and our ministry, in order to allow them to fulfill their potential – even if it means they move on to another ministry, under another's leadership?

## Reproducing and Releasing Leaders

This is why it is so important for us, if we truly want to become extraordinary leaders, to remember that whatever church or ministry we lead actually belongs to the Lord, not to us. As we reproduce leadership, the positioning of those leaders is ultimately to give Him the most glory and accomplish the most for His Kingdom, not ours.

There is a great challenge in being true Godly leaders of impact. It is time for church and ministry leadership to step up to active, unselfish leadership reproduction.

When we are willing to humble ourselves, share the revelations and insights into leadership that God has given us, and sacrifice some time to help others develop their leadership potential – even if it is eventually to be used to fulfill the vision God has given another - there is no limit to how far-reaching, long-lasting, and widespread the impact of our leadership can become.

## Chapter 13
## NURTURING AND USING GOD'S GIFTS

The Word tells us that God has given the five-fold ministry to His people for the edifying of the body, with the goal of all of us becoming more Christ-like:

*"And he gave some, apostles; and some, prophets; and some, evangelists; and some, pastors and teachers; for the perfecting of the saints, for the work of the ministry, for the edifying of the body of Christ: Till we all come in the unity of the faith, and of the knowledge of the Son of God, unto a perfect man, unto the measure of the stature of the fulness of Christ."* (Eph. 4:11-13)

We must be mindful, as influencers called to one or more of the five-fold ministry positions, to stir, encourage, and raise up others with the same calling. But we must never forget that the gifts of God do not begin and end with the five-fold ministry.

While most Christian leaders work with a few potential leaders in whom they recognize a five-fold calling, it is sadly too often to the neglect of stirring the other diverse giftings of the Holy Spirit laying dormant in the average believer.

**It Begins With Us**

One key factor in reproducing leaders is learning how to recognize, acknowledge, and help develop the God-given gifts of all of those over whom you have been given authority.

It will begin with us, as leaders, learning, developing and becoming comfortable with the gifts and anointings God has given each of us personally. That confidence in knowing who God has called us to be will make us able to willingly promote the giftings of others – even if they differ from those we operate in.

We discussed earlier the necessity to conquer our fears in order to be extraordinary leaders who will impact others to lead. One of the fears that has crippled the body of Christ is the fear that someone we lead might become more powerful in some areas than we are. How easily our natural pride keeps us from remembering that the Word tells us that each manifestation is for everyone's benefit, is the responsibility of the Holy Spirit, not of the person operating in the gift, and that God is the one that determines who needs which gift to fulfill His purposes.

*"But the manifestation of the Spirit is given to every man to profit withal. For to one is given by the Spirit the word of wisdom; to another the word of knowledge by the same Spirit; to another faith by the same Spirit; to another the gifts of healing by the same Spirit; to another the working of miracles; to another prophecy; to another discerning of spirits; to another divers kinds of tongues; to another the interpretation of tongues: But all these worketh that one and the selfsame Spirit, dividing to every man severally as he will."* (1 Cor. 12:7-11)

**Confidence in Our Call**

How can we teach those we lead that they need never be jealous, envious, or covetous of any other believer's specific gifts and callings if we ourselves can't mature past that kind of carnal thinking. We must first know deep in our own hearts that God has a specific plan for our individual lives, leaders or not, and that the gifts He gives us are those He knows we will need to fulfill His plan. When we know this we can joyfully watch God bring forth the giftings He has planned for someone else, and even help in the process.

As Christian leaders, we must remember that our prime responsibility is to lead others into maturity. But Paul goes on in Ephesians, after identifying the five-fold ministry gifts and their goal of equipping the saints, to remind us that the true importance of raising the saints to maturity is the

## Nurturing and Using God's Gifts

protection it will bring them from being deceived and pulled away from God's plan for their life:

*"That we henceforth be no more children, tossed to and fro, and carried about with every wind of doctrine, by the sleight of men, and cunning craftiness, whereby they lie in wait to deceive."* (Eph. 4:14)

Once we have grown in Him, conquered our own insecurities by learning to walk in the spirit and not in the flesh, and taken a leadership role, it is time to begin to recognize, acknowledge, nurture and put to use the gifts God has given us in the people we lead.

After all, our giftings all come from the same God, who wants the very best for each of us, and who knows which of His glorious gifts we need to do all He has for each of us:

*"Now there are diversities of gifts, but the same Spirit. And there are differences of administrations, but the same Lord. And there are diversities of operations, but it is the same God which worketh all in all."* (1 Cor. 12:4-6)

**Advancing in the Gifts**

As we set out, operating in the gifts He has given us, He will often expand those giftings. We need to be prepared to readjust our thinking and our actions as more and more gifts are activated.

Take me, for example. Since I have predominantly moved in the anointing of prophecy, I have trained many people to move in this supernatural anointing of the Lord. However, as God advanced me through prayer and the exercising of the anointing He's placed in me, I have begun to get words of knowledge and am now seeing the gift of healing manifest in my ministry.

After being blessed to see the Lord heal one member of our congregation with heart problems and another with severe joint pain, I realized that I could also help others move into this healing gift too, as well as encouraging them to discover whatever other spiritual gifts He may have for their lives.

In my ministry training sessions I began to speak the Scriptures, such as Mark 16, and remind them of the power of the believers' anointing we discussed earlier. As people were encouraged and their gifts were nurtured, they became emboldened and began to move out in their giftings.

They learned that as they sought God, used their prayer language, and learned to hear and obey what He was saying through His Holy Spirit, they could be used and see Him manifest Himself whenever He chose, even on the streets doing evangelism.

**Seeking Instructions & Opportunities**

They learned to seek Him for opportunities to use their gifts in practical ways, even in day-to-day living, asking, "God, how would you manifest yourself to help this unbeliever at this hour?" or "God, how will you use me to manifest your power on my job and help this person who is suffering?"

We need to raise up others to seek God's instructions in prayer and then use the tools, the gifts, He has given them to follow those instructions. As leaders we are to expect those whom we are mentoring to be able to be used in the believers anointing, because the Word of God says, "those who believe" shall do these things. We need to help them discover that these promises are for them.

*"So we, being many, are one body in Christ, and every one members one of another. Having then gifts differing according to the grace that is given to us, whether prophecy, let us prophesy according to the proportion of faith; Or ministry, let us wait on our ministering: or he that teacheth, on teaching; Or he that exhorteth, on exhortation: he that giveth, let him do it with simplicity;*

*he that ruleth, with diligence; he that sheweth mercy, with cheerfulness."* (Rom. 12:5-8 )

Then we must seek God as to how we can best help them step out in their giftings. A true impact leader will be sure that those they lead are taught proper Biblical operation of gifts. Then they must be given opportunities to put their giftings in practice, even allowing for mistakes and misunderstandings as they grow and develop the full operation of their God-given gifts.

**Covet to Prophesy**

As a leader, even if we are not called to the office of the prophet, we must desire to prophesy over the destinies, callings, and giftings of those we lead. Perhaps it is because the prophetic is so vital in helping others to recognize, acknowledge and be launched into their destiny that Paul admonished us, in I Cor. 14:39, to "covet to prophesy."

So that those we lead can mature, we leaders must mature, becoming more desirous to lay hands on others, as the Holy Spirit leads, and imparting into them that which has been given to us in order to see them fulfill their destinies and callings.

Being humble enough to want to see those we lead grow into the fullness of what God has for them, and leading them into boldly acknowledging and using their gifts will make us the kind of extraordinary leaders who will make an impact in our church, our home, our job, our community, the nation, and the world.

## Chapter 14
## IMPACTING CHILDREN AND YOUTH

Reaching, teaching and leading the teens and the children is a special call and anointing.

If you are a pastor or leader in a ministry that includes young people and children, you have a grave responsibility to provide quality called and anointed leadership for their classes and for programs geared to their needs.

Although every mature believer, and certainly every active leader, can be led of the Holy Ghost to touch the needs of anyone put before them, not every called leader, or potential leader, is truly gifted in working with God's little ones. It is the specific call and destiny for some leaders.

In a ministry called to make an impact on all ages and ethnic groups, the children and young people must be challenged to submit, commit, and keep growing in the Lord, much as the adults are. It must be done at a level they can comprehend, but never forgetting that when a 7-year old gives their heart to the Lord and receives the infilling of the Holy Spirit, the power they receive is the same power an adult receives – the same Spirit that raised Christ from the dead, dwelling in them.

A true impact leader will never settle long for "someone to keep the children occupied," or "someone who can relate to teens and give them something to do." Instead, he or she will pray in or raise up a leader for them who is called and anointed by God to raise the young ones up into young warriors.

The ministry I founded through the Lord Jesus Christ has trained youth in the ministry of the prophetic. A testimony from one of the young teens blessed the congregation as she said, "I really appreciate this ministry because I thought ministry was only for adults. But because I am in training and have the opportunity to serve, I am grateful for how God has used me, as well. It has given me vision and purpose."

**Reach Instead of Rescue**

The more called and anointed leaders of youth and children who take their God-given places will mean more little ones being reached early and fewer having to be "rescued" by our adult counselors or prison ministry leaders later. That is true impact leadership.

Conversely, if your ministry, or area of leadership does not include youth and children you should be watchful among the potential leaders you are raising up for those who have this special gift. If you do not have a need for this specific gifting in your ministry, it is your responsibility to raise that person up in leadership and then be willing to release them to use what they have learned in another ministry where their specific gift can be used to the fullest.

This way you are impacting young people and children with your life by raising up those who will help lead them to maturity in Christ.

As you bless another's ministry by releasing a gifted teen or children's leader to take a position, God will always bless you with another leader better suited to fill the position you need filled. After all, He has a called, anointed, and appointed person for every necessary position in His vision for the ministry He has called you to lead.

## Chapter 15
## INITIATING CHANGE & EMBRACING THE NEW

We've determined that being a good example of the character of Christ is an important part of being an exceptional leader. It is being that good example that makes others willing to follow your lead.

Of course, there will always be some who come who are drawn to your anointing and yet have no intention of following your leadership, no matter what. But, because you are committed and demonstrate Jesus so well, others will desire to follow, and you can initiate change by your example.

Why is it important to have people trust you and be willing to follow when you initiate change? Because our Heavenly Father initiates by change. As impact leaders we need to be hearing His voice and knowing when God is initiating change. Then we need to be willing to embrace the new as He moves us forward.

In my ministry to God, determined to follow Him and to do His will, I have found that there are those who say they want change, and believe they are walking in the new, when, in fact, traditional cords continue to hold them back. It is our role to do whatever they will allow us to do toward helping them break those bonds.

We need to have the foresight to see what's coming as God is shifting things, positioning circumstances, or repositioning His people. We need to be able to seek Him and find out what He's doing, because He is always doing something. He's always moving - changing what has been and shifting it into another method which will work better for today.

God is calling for the church to begin to move forward with great expediency; pressing full speed ahead into the new. Moses and Aaron understood this principle: *"And Samuel said unto the people, It is the LORD that advanced Moses and Aaron, and that brought your fathers up out of the land of Egypt."* (1 Sam. 12:6)

## Moving With God Is Vital

Moses caught the vision God had given him, that showed him that in order for Israel to advance into the new they had to come out of captivity; and stop surviving on the maintenance mentality which had blocked their progress. God desired to take them into a deeper walk together and with Him.

The hard part of being aware of the changes God is making is that it could very well mean we must change the way we've always done things.

But keeping up with the move of God is vital, because you can't stay in the old and walk into the future with Him. Moving with Him is necessary to fully accomplish His desire for both yourself and those you will impact.

Your confidence in knowing God's will when it is necessary to initiate major changes will give those you lead the confidence to follow you into the future.

Good leaders recognize when they are on target and when they are caught in the old and need to shift and seek God for the new. To be on track with God it is sometimes necessary to take something we already have and let Him make it into something else.

## Obedience Brings Advancement

When you read in the book of Genesis about the life of Abraham you see one good example of a leader who initiated change.

More than once the Lord gave Him instructions that meant dropping everything and moving on to a whole new life. God

## Initiating Change and Embracing the New

gave him a prophetic word and as Abraham moved out in obedience, God gave another order.

Because He was devoted to the Lord, he was obedient. That devotion and obedience made him an extraordinary leader who earned the accolade "father of the faithful."

This kind of leader must be willing to act out the marching orders he's been given, and exercise his/her part in moving the church or ministry forward.

Joshua is another prime example of an extraordinary leader. He issued an alarm to the people to advance. He had to face the fact that Moses was gone and it was up to him to lead the Israelites into the promised land after 40 years of wandering in the desert. Now that was initiating change!

The word "progress" means to advance, to make headway. Can you hear the call to advance? Can't you sense it in the spiritual airwaves? As an impact leader it will be up to you to issue the call to advance and initiate the change that will take your vision, and those God has called around you, into the future.

True leaders, being guided by the Holy Spirit, determine not only when to build, but when to leave the scaffolding up and for how long, what to replace, and what to leave in the original state. They determine when to hold ground and when to advance.

**Progress Requires Trust**

When you are called to build it is important to seek God on who is to come alongside. These are the ones for whom you will lay down your life.

Those who are following their lead will be able to make progress, move with the flow and adjust to the changes involved when they have trust in their leader to initiate wisely.

Sometimes the changes can be painful. After all, our carnal nature does not like things to change. But again the positive, confident attitude of the person leading will impact those going through the challenges with you.

It is important to be willing to initiate change because change is a step of progression. Think of the negative impact if Joshua had not been willing to initiate change!

We must be willing to progress, move forward.

In the book of Acts, the disciples and others who followed Jesus Christ were willing to progress or they would not have waited in the upper room all those days. After all, they had no precedent for doing this. They were being asked to do something that they had never even heard of, let alone experienced.

To take this step, they had to walk in the spirit, not the flesh, because their carnal minds had to have told them it was absurd, even crazy.

**Stepping Into the Unexpected**

Therefore those who waited in the upper room had to be totally confident of the One who had led them to do this. They had to trust Him. They had to become focused, fixed and steadfast waiting for the Holy Spirit to come even though they didn't know quite what to expect.

Jesus Christ had told them He was going to ask the Father to send the Holy Spirit, but they didn't really know what that meant. Remember, up to that time they had only known Jesus, so they couldn't know the operations of the Holy Spirit without Him. As they waited, steadfast and immovable, they were trusting in Jesus because they had seen the faithfulness and integrity of His leadership.

God saw their trust, heard their prayer for all He had for them, and sent his promised Holy Spirit as they waited.

**Progress Brings Harvest**

After the Holy Spirit had come, they were able to move out, to advance, to begin fulfilling His plan. It was through that change, and their willingness to progress into the next

## Initiating Change and Embracing the New

phase of God's plan for them that God's reproduction system was launched.

The result was a great harvest of souls on fire for Jesus:

*"Then they that gladly received his word were baptized: and the same day there were added unto them about three thousand souls. they continued stedfastly in the apostles' doctrine and fellowship, and in breaking of bread, and in prayers."* (Acts 2:41-42)

Trusting the one who was leading, so much so that they were willing to die to their flesh and let the Holy Spirit lead them into change, was a must for the disciples in the upper room. As an impact leader you too must show those over whom you have been given authority that you are being led of the Holy Spirit and can be trusted.

**Embrace the New**

God is continually illuminating something new in Scripture for us to embrace to take us farther into progression. A person who desires to make an impact for Jesus Christ must be willing to leave the old and embrace the new.

*"Call unto me, and I will answer thee, and shew thee great and mighty things, which thou knowest not."* (Jer. 33:3)

As a leader you must instill the confidence of your calling into those you lead so that they will be willing to follow you into the new. You must teach them to continue to look forward and to move willingly when change is initiated so they will not miss the next blessing God has for them as they progress with the vision God has given you, as the leader, to fulfill.

As you embrace the new together, you must be totally persuaded, and then persuade them, that God has promised to make the way. When God says to change, stop, or shift, we must never listen to man; only to Him. I can advise you, from personal experience, to have wise counsel only from

## Becoming an Extraordinary Leader

those more mature in the faith and ministry. It is not wise to get counsel from those who are less mature than yourself.

*"Remember ye not the former things, neither consider the things of old. Behold, I will do a new thing; now it shall spring forth; shall ye not know it? I will even make a way in the wilderness, and rivers in the desert."* (Isa. 43:18-19)

Our progressive steps reinforce the deposit of grace and vision to those around us

### Progress Is Worth the Risk

Progress means allowing advancement to take place in spite of the mistakes that might be made. It means giving up that with which you may have become very comfortable for the uncertainty of the next step. It may mean risking relationships with those who are not willing to move with us or continue to help us if we make the change.

In order to move forward we must be willing to take chances, trusting the Holy Spirit that is leading us to initiate the change, and knowing that His "new thing" is worth the risk.

### The Risk of Impact Leadership

If you determine to be a good leader, remember, impact leaders risk more than others think is comfortable. If you never take chances, you will never progress, never advance into kingdom purposes. Instead you will simply maintain and become dull and stagnant. Stagnant waters smell and kill off what ever life might have been in it. Waters that keep moving are full of life.

God desires to release "rivers of living waters" within us so that we may be a refreshing to others.

Be prepared, as a leader, to accept the leading of the Holy Spirit when He indicates that changes are necessary and then initiate change boldly and confidently, risking losing the "status quo" to initiate something new, something life-giving.

## Initiating Change and Embracing the New

As those who are under your authority watch you make the transition with peace and assurance, even if it is a rocky one, you will find them working alongside you. Then you can move together, leading them one step of progress at a time, toward the future and the fulfillment of the ministry vision He has given you.

"Pressing toward the goal for the prize" in Jesus, as Paul said in the book of Philippians, is not always easy. That's why he admonishes us to press.

## Chapter 16
## WALKING TOGETHER IN MEMBERSHIP MINISTRY

To become a successful Christian leader, one must be delivered from the crowd to become a leader of the crowd. But, an extraordinary leader, one with notable impact on others' lives, is gracious and desires to do what is necessary within reason to keep the morale of those partaking in the vision high.

A true leader must know how to create an atmosphere of "team player," encouraging membership ministry, while still maintaining their authority as a leader.

There will be those who say they are team players, when in actuality their "Lone Ranger" mentality can be seen. Focus your anointing on those who are truly willing to become joined up – those willing to make a united effort to accomplish God's work.

### Strong Sense of Fulfillment

Membership ministry is simply acknowledgment that we are a member of the body of Christ with each one carrying the portion of supply God has placed within us to help His Body be a live organism. As believers move in their membership ministry, they develop a strong sense of fulfillment for their lives. They begin to feel useful and vital to what God is doing. This fulfillment motivates them to seek out greater vision from our Heavenly Father. The cycle continues as it sets His people on course.

It is one thing to agree in theory to the idea of teamwork and unity. It is another thing to put it into practice. Walking together takes patience and forgiveness. If we are to truly become team players and encourage others to become team players there must be a mentoring anointing flowing.

## Progress Requires Trust

When the ones we are leading see that we are willing to stick it out and continue to walk with them during their mistakes, shortcomings, and lack of maturity it will teach them to do the same with others.

Unfortunately, there are those who will not always do the same for you. This is one of the areas where humility plays such a large part, and which emphasizes the importance of humility in an impact leader.

Corporate leaders in the world tend to stay aloof, being "larger than life", and keeping a totally different lifestyle and set of standards than what they expect from their "underlings." But that is the world. It ought not to be so in the church. Again, we have Jesus as the example, and we have the Holy Spirit to direct us, so we have no excuse for falling back into the prideful, arrogant ways of the world.

## Pride Goes Before Destruction

Proverbs warns us:

*"Pride goeth before destruction, and a haughty spirit before a fall."* (Prov. 16:18)

Sadly, there are churches and ministries today which have been destroyed, and men and women of God, once great leaders, who have fallen away from the Lord.

They let the worldly ideas feed their carnal pride, make them feel "larger than life," or to behave as though they had a special dispensation from God to live in the worldly ways they taught their followers to shun.

Once again we must be reminded that as leaders making an impact for the Kingdom of God we must apply God's standards, not the worlds, if we are to succeed and fulfill His call on our lives.

## Activating the Five-Fold Ministry

And as chosen leaders, a part of our destiny will be to lead those God has entrusted to our leadership into a true membership ministry, with those called to five-fold ministry being raised up and empowered and all believers pulling together, doing their part, to bring in the end-time harvest.

As impact leaders we must be proactive in stirring and utilizing the gifts of those God has called into the five-fold ministry.

For too long it has been necessary for saints who are hungry for more of the Lord to seek out special conferences and seminars in order to sit under a called prophet or evangelist.

It is crucial that we begin to see the five-fold ministry gifts - apostles, prophets, evangelist, pastors and teachers - activated in the local church because that is the foundation God has set up for the purposes of equipping and training the saints. As leaders it is our responsibility to see to it.

It is the responsibility of the five-fold ministry gifts to tear down strongholds, shift His Church from a mass of apathetic babies "playing church" on Sunday into strong, active warriors for the Lord, knowing how to occupy and possess.

These extraordinary leaders will invite, raise up, and encourage those operating in the five-fold ministry gifts to work alongside them, and together they will teach the saints how to move forward together as a team in unity, fulfilling their membership ministry.

## Unity Among Churches and Ministries

It is important for leaders to motivate unity, activate membership ministry, and develop a "team" player attitude in those they lead. But remember that much of leadership is done by example.

One important part of leading your followers into true understanding of the importance of unity is to see unity between you, as their leader, and other churches, ministries, and leaders.

If we are teaching, and prayerfully we are, that there is a God-given destiny for each believer and a God-given vision for each church and ministry, then we need never be "in competition" with, or jealous of, any other person's or ministry's growth or success.

Instead we should be "rejoicing with those that rejoice" as the Bible teaches us (see Rom. 12:15). Therefore we should never hesitate to support another church's activity, allow our members to visit and glean from another's revelation, etc.

**The Witness of Unity**

What a glorious witness it is to the unsaved in a community when a group of churches or ministries get together and host an outreach to needy children, or put together a conference where leaders and members from several participating groups praise, pray and grow together!

Fortunately, there is a growing desire among leaders to learn how to walk together and serve one another, exemplifying unity for this great call the Lord has upon us, and we need to encourage it and become a part of it.

There is much Biblical basis for such unity. For example, Moses and Aaron not only had to learn to walk together, but how to incorporate and walk side by side with the seventy elders and priests.

**Why Jesus Prayed for Unity**

I feel confident that such unity will come to pass in the body of Christ in this end-time. If we expect God to answer our prayers, how much more can we expect Him to answer Jesus' prayers. Let's consider Jesus' prayer for His disciples and for us:

> *"Neither pray I for these alone, but for them also which shall believe on me through their word; That they all may be one; as thou, Father, art in me, and I in thee,*

*that they also may be one in us: that the world may believe that thou hast sent me. And the glory which thou gavest me I have given them; that they may be one, even as we are one: I in them, and thou in me, that they may be made perfect in one; and that the world may know that thou hast sent me, and hast loved them, as thou hast loved me."* (John 17:20-23)

Notice the ultimate reason that Jesus felt it was important for us to be in unity – so that the world would know that God had sent Him.

If unity among the believers is such a vital key to harvest, it is no wonder that the enemy has worked so hard, largely using our fear and pride, to keep believers divided. He has succeeded far too long! It is time for us, as leaders, to break the stronghold of division and build the bridge of unity, first walking together with those we lead, and then joining hands and joining forces with others who love the Lord and are determined to accomplish His purpose in His way.

**Preparing for Victory**

We're preparing to be one of the greatest generations that ever lived. No generation has the destiny that this one faces. It is inclusive of fresh revelation from God, demonstration of the Holy Spirit manifested through mankind, evangelism and practical application for those serving Jesus Christ in their workplace.

As joint heirs with Jesus Christ (Rom. 8:17), we are being prepared to be co-laborers with Him for His eternal purposes (1 Cor. 3:9). We are to wait for His marching orders. While waiting, we're to become equipped ourselves by the study of the Word of God and spending time with the Lord. As He develops our heart and brings us more and more revelation, we are to take our position of leadership, put our hands to the plow, and walk our daily destiny.

But we do not walk it alone. We walk as co-laborers with the Lord Himself, alongside our brothers and sisters in Christ

– an unbeatable army marching into battle to take the victory for Jesus!

# HEART TO HEART
## A Personal Closing Word From Jimmie Reed

As an extraordinary leader, one who is seeking to bring others into the fullness of their calling, you will lay down your life for others in ways they will never completely understand.

While it is a highly rewarding calling, it will not always be an easy walk.

Having been one to serve other ministers to help build and establish, as well as being a leader in the body of Christ, I can tell you that even with the best intentions to trust, train up others and release them, it will not always work out the way you hope.

I have laid hands on too soon and even suffered great loss in different areas of ministry and my personal life. Many will speak of desires and a vision that they will never seek to accomplish, and as a visionary you will be drawn in only to find you are alone.

Sometimes it will even be the very ones you sacrificed for the most, those you trusted and held dear to your own heart, those in whom you have invested greatly, who will (for any number of reasons) end up taking you for granted, and you may even lose authority, vision, and purpose in their sight.

Even when you diligently seek the Lord on who to invest in and it is mutually agreed upon, there are many different reasons why it doesn't always work out His way. Whether you somehow missed it or the error was on the part of the ones whom you felt called to, God is still in charge. As leaders who train, we must be careful because we too are human and can hurt. We must determine to die to our fleshly hurts and disappointments, forgive, and keep moving forward.

As a man or woman called by God to be a leader who impacts the body of Christ, you must know that there is still no greater reward for one personally than to see others moving toward achieving what God has ordained them to do.

Each life that you are able to impact, each person you are able to boost to another level toward fulfilling their God-given destiny, is worth all the sacrifice, all the challenges, that will come your way, knowing we will be rewarded by Christ as we are faithful. He is the Master of all.

## ABOUT THE AUTHOR
## Dr. Jimmie Reed

An extraordinary leader herself, Jimmie Reed's call is to bring others into the fullness of their calling, by equipping, activating, and imparting the depth of revelation and insight the Lord has given her in the Word.

Having served the Lord since age 24, Jimmie has a degree from the Christian Life School of Theology, was ordained both by Pastor Dutch Sheets, Springs Harvest Fellowship, and Bishop Bill Hamon, president and founder of Christian International Apostolic Network, and received her master's and doctorate degrees in practical ministry from Wagner Leadership Institute.

Jimmie is founder and president of Jimmie Reed Ministries, as well as Eagles International Leadership Training School and School of the Prophets. She is widely sought-after, both across the US and in the nations of the world as a conference speaker and seminar teacher, as well as for her powerful prophetic ministry.

She has been featured on both Trinity Broadcasting and Daystar Television Networks, and has a local weekly television program, "Your Day of Breakthrough." Her first book, *Who Me, Prophesy?* was published in 2004 by Xulon Press.

Headquartered in Colorado, Jimmie is the mother of four grown children, as well as a spiritual mother, covering or advisor to dozens of men and women she has raised up and equipped for ministry.

## ABOUT JIMMIE REED MINISTRIES
### Eagle International Schools of Ministry, Schools of the Prophets & Holy Spirit Seminars

୭୧

Jimmie Reed Ministries (JRM), founded in 1998, is a ministry called of God to teach, train, and equip the saints for the work of the ministry. This ministry carries a strong anointing of activation and impartation to help others increase in their gifts.

The founder and president of JRM, Dr. Jimmie Reed has a heart to demystify the prophetic, as well as operate in a reproducing anointing to bring others to new levels for their everyday lives and their specific callings.

To fulfill this call, JRM offers Eagles International Leadership Training Schools, Schools of the Prophets, and Holy Spirit Seminars.

### EAGLES INTERNATIONAL LEADERSHIP TRAINING SCHOOLS

JRM sponsors Eagles International Leadership Training Schools across the nation, based on Ephesians 2:19-20. These non-traditional schools have been developed to train and equip the Body of Christ by offering innovative courses to establish, impart, and minister to students while offering insight into the moving of God on the earth today.

Eagles' courses are taught by highly respected men and women of God, with years of experience in leadership and expertise in the subjects offered.

Both short-term and long-term programs are offered and a variety of certificates may be earned through the Eagles International Leadership Training Schools.

The Eagles Curriculum includes, but is not limited to, courses in: Ministering Spiritual Gifts; Hitting the Mark; Godly Character; Prophetic Pitfalls; Prophets and Personal Prophecy; Prophets and the Prophetic Movement; Dreams and Visions; Understanding the Anointing; Intercessory prayer; Prophetic Intercession; Apostolic Intercession; Effective Speaking; Pulpit Etiquette; Protocol for Ministry; Prophetic Evangelism; Personal Ministry; Becoming an Impact Leader; God's Armor Bearer; The Eagle Life; Marketplace Ministry; Apostles and God's Apostolic Movement; Pastoral Studies; and Healing.

## JRM SCHOOL OF THE PROPHETS

The JRM School of the Prophets is designed for those who desire to gain a greater understanding of how the prophetic is applied today.

This school is taught primarily by Prophet Jimmie Reed, but on occasion she will be assisted by other well respected men and women of God who operate in and have great knowledge of the prophetic.

Subjects covered in these schools include: Who Me, Prophesy?; Ministering Spiritual Gifts; Prophets, Pitfalls and Principles; Prophets and Personal Prophecy; and Hitting the Mark & Godly Character.

## GATHERING OF EAGLES
## LEADERSHIP SEMINARS

Gathering of Eagles Leadership Seminars are opportunities for those in apostolic/prophetic leadership in an area to come together to be edified and equipped to embrace the fullness of their God-given call.

Highly respected and anointed ministry leaders join Apostle Jimmie to lead these times of deep teaching and revelation, and to impart their expertise to enrich leaders at all levels.

## HOLY SPIRIT SEMINARS

Holy Spirit Seminars are gatherings, usually held monthly, to bring together the saints in a local area to be stirred, encouraged, and better equipped in the gifts of the Holy Spirit.

Times of powerfully anointed corporate praise and worship is followed by encouragement and edification from the Word of God. Personal prayer is offered for attendees, and the JRM Prophetic Presbytery is available at the end of the service to seek the Lord for prophetic encouragement for those individuals wanting a personal touch from the Lord.

Holy Spirit Seminars are currently being held monthly in Denver, Colorado and the Santa Fe, New Mexico areas.

**For more information regarding attending or hosting Holy Spirit Seminars, Schools of the Prophets or Eagle International Leadership Training Schools in your area, please contact:**

        **Jimmie Reed Ministries**
        **PO Box 63582**
        **Colorado Springs, CO 80962**
        **719-599-4477**
        **www.jimmiereedmin.org**

## ABOUT THE EDITOR
### Roxanne Ryan



Roxanne Ryan, founder of *His Voice / His Pen Ministries*, is an ordained minister who teaches, preaches, writes, and edits Christian material. She has ministered in churches and conferences in the U.S., Canada, and Nigeria, and writes and edits for numerous international Christian ministries and evangelists.

Her recent works include: "Still God's Little Girl," the biography of Angie Brogan; "Hang in There – Your Today is Not Your Forever," the biography of Francis Moore; and "Light at the End of the Tunnel," co-authored with Ron Schueler. She is co-author, with Rev. Claudia Garr, of the seminar series "Journey to Triumphant Living".

Roxanne is a member of Word of Life Christian Center in Lone Tree, Colorado, Dr. Mark T. Bagwell, pastor. She also serves on the Board of Directors and Ministry Teams of *Redeemed Ones International Ministries*; *Covenant House of Love Ministries*; and *Healing Waters Ministries*.

She formerly served on the ministry team at Blood Covenant Christian Faith Center in Pomona, California, and as Associate Editor of Publications and Testimony Director for *Morris Cerullo World Evangelism*, San Diego, California.

# OTHER POWERFUL MINISTRY TOOLS AVAILABLE FROM JRM

ം

## AUDIO TAPE SERIES

### *Moving in Apostolic Authority*

There is a releasing of the former rain with the latter rain during this season. This series unlocks the mysteries of moving in apostolic authority.

### *Becoming a Person of Destiny*

Discover the destiny God has for your life - learn to "think destiny" for yourself and others.

### *Double Portion*

The Lord desires for the church to operate in all the power He has given her. Learn how to appropriate His *Double Portion*.

### *Transition: A Season of Change*

We are all moving from one place to another place in the Lord. These tapes will help you make the most of your new season.

### *Apostolic & Prophetic Intercession*

God wants His people to have victory over the enemy. This series shows you His plan for seeing it come to pass.

### *I Will Build My Church*

Learn how Jesus Christ promises to build us individually to help us to stand together corporately.

### *The Miraculous Church*

For a miraculous church every saint must be activated into all God has for them. Hear how God Himself will bring it to pass.

# MORE POWERFUL MINISTRY TOOLS AVAILABLE FROM JRM

## AUDIOTAPE SERIES (cont.)

### Empowerment For Breakthrough

God has called a people of breakthrough. This series will equip you to be all He has called you to be.

### Operating in Your Gifts

This series will help you to lead a more disciplined life while God develops a determination in you to mature your character.

## BOOKS

### Who, Me Prophesy?

An easy to read book designed to cut through all the confusion, fear and mystery surrounding prophecy and show each believer the role prophecy can have in their own lives.

## TO ORDER CONTACT:

**Jimmie Reed Ministries**
**PO Box 63582**
**Colorado Springs, CO 80962**
**719-599-4477**
www.jimmiereedmin.org

www.ingramcontent.com/pod-product-compliance
Lightning Source LLC
Chambersburg PA
CBHW071405160426
42813CB00084B/506